OFFENSIVE BASEBALL DRILLS

OFFENSIVE BASEBALL DRILLS

Rod Delmonico
Head Baseball Coach, University of Tennessee

Human Kinetics

Library of Congress Cataloging-in-Publication Data

Delmonico, Rod, 1958-
    Offensive baseball drills / Rod Delmonico.
      p. cm.
    ISBN 0-87322-865-0
    1. Baseball--Training. 2. Baseball--Offense. I. Title.
  GV875.6.D45 1996
  796.357'07--dc20   95-42628
                                                  CIP

ISBN: 0-87322-865-0

Developmental Editor: Marni Basic; **Assistant Editor:** Susan Moore; **Editorial Assistant:** Jennifer J. Hemphill; **Copyeditor:** Jacqueline Eaton Blakley; **Proofreader:** Bob Replinger; **Typesetter and Layout Artist:** Francine Hamerski; **Text Designer:** Stuart Cartwright; **Photo Editor:** Boyd LaFoon; **Cover Designer:** Jack Davis; **Photographer (cover):** Nick Myers; **Photographer (interior):** Nick Myers and Lisa Glanton; **Illustrator:** Studio 2-D; **Printer:** United Graphics

Human Kinetics books are available at special discounts for bulk purchase. Special editions or book excerpts can also be created to specification. For details, contact the Special Sales Manager at Human Kinetics.

Printed in the United States of America   10 9 8 7 6 5 4 3 2 1

Human Kinetics
P.O. Box 5076, Champaign, IL 61825-5076
1-800-747-4457

Canada: Human Kinetics, Box 24040, Windsor, ON N8Y 4Y9
1-800-465-7301 (in Canada only)

Europe: Human Kinetics, P.O. Box IW14, Leeds LS16 6TR, United Kingdom
(44) 1132 781708

Australia: Human Kinetics, 2 Ingrid Street, Clapham 5062, South Australia
(08) 371 3755

New Zealand: Human Kinetics, P.O. Box 105-231, Auckland 1
(09) 523 3462

To all the children who love the game of baseball,
especially my three sons Tony, Joey, and Nicky.

Contents

• • • • • • • • • • • • • • • •

Foreword

· · · · · · · · · · · · · · · · · ·

Scoring runs doesn't just happen by accident. Baseball players and teams who score a lot do so because they have a variety of offensive weapons in their arsenal. They hit for average, hit for power, and hit behind the runner. They bunt to get on base and bunt to sacrifice. They run the bases effectively and get their share of steals.

The ability to execute a variety of skills is essential to being an offensive threat. A player or team who can do only one or two things well is much easier for the defense to stop. And you're in big trouble when you're more likely to score on opponents' errors than with your offense.

Some coaches are great teachers of offensive baseball. One such coach is Rod Delmonico. One of the best young coaches in the game, Rod has built his University of Tennessee baseball program into a national power.

Rod believes in aggressive baseball—forcing the action, not laying back and waiting for a big inning that may never happen. That philosophy is obvious in the way that he teaches and drills his players.

In *Offensive Baseball Drills*, Rod presents 68 practice drills that make you more productive at the plate and better on the base paths. The key points that accompany each drill are especially valuable for skill development. The information and sample practice plans in the last chapter show you how to use the drills, regardless of age or ability. This book is a perfect practice tool.

Make your practices more fun and more productive with *Offensive Baseball Drills*. If you practice these drills regularly and pay attention to Rod's special tips, you'll see results—in the scorebook!

Tommy Lasorda
Manager, Los Angeles Dodgers

Acknowledgments

In addition to many coaching colleagues and players who unknowingly helped to find the parameters for the contents of this book, I would like to give special thanks to my wife Barb and my secretary Janie Cormack, who spent countless hours typing the manuscript and to several of my players posing for pictures and also to the staff in whole, especially Ted Miller and Marni Basic, who helped to make this book possible.

Introduction

Introduction

Pitching is said to be 70 to 90 percent of baseball in terms of who wins and who loses. But if you have a consistent, run-producing offense, you're never out of a game.

The more runs you produce, the more excitement, notoriety, and—most important—wins you generate. This is especially true at the collegiate level, where two factors—the designated hitter and aluminum bats—favor run production. Factor in mediocre pitching (there are only so many good arms to go around), and it's no wonder so many winning collegiate teams point to a strong and consistent offense as the main reason for their success.

At the University of Tennessee, scoring runs consistently is a big factor in our success. The same was true of the Florida State teams I worked with as an assistant coach before becoming head coach at Tennessee.

Hitting and scoring are infectious. A leadoff base hit offers hope of a big inning. Another hit puts runners at first and third and your team has a little rally going. That little rally becomes a big one, and all of a sudden that two-run deficit becomes a three-run lead. With a potent offensive lineup, apparent losses can become come-from-behind victories.

The key is to develop a *consistent* offense. Almost any team can mount a rally now and then. But teams that are physically and mentally prepared to hit, run, take the extra base, steal, and score, *expect* to score every inning. Consistent offensive teams are like machines—they manufacture runs.

The ability to produce runs consistently comes from smart, hard practice. Building a high-powered offense takes serious dedication that begins with the coach and filters down to the last player on the bench. It takes knowing *how* to perform skills like the hit-and-run, the squeeze, the double steal, and the back-door slide, and knowing *when* to use those skills or put those plays on.

Offensive Baseball Drills provides practice activities that will help you learn and develop all of the skills needed to be a consistent threat at the plate and on the base paths. The 68 drills in this book will help players at all levels develop the fundamentals of offensive play—hitting, bunting, stealing, and running the bases. All of the drills provide special tips, and several include more difficult variations.

Chapters 1 and 2 focus on hitting and baserunning skills, respectively. In chapter 3, the emphasis shifts from individual skill development to more tactical team drills. Here you will find a drill for almost every game situation. These are key practice activities for preparing for an opponent and developing a better feel for baseball strategy.

My practice recommendations in chapter 4 will help you organize your workouts to best apply the drills from the first three chapters. The sample practice plans in this section might be particularly helpful.

Every drill in this book is a part of the puzzle, with the big picture being how to score more runs. You'll learn drills that effectively teach how to get on base, advance, and cross home plate. And in executing the drills, players will develop more than just the physical skills required to be good offensive players—they'll develop the mental aggressiveness it takes to manufacture runs on a regular basis.

In my book, a run's a run, whether it comes from a base hit, home run, walk, steal, or sacrifice. It counts the same in the scorebook. The idea is to score runs any way you can and not leave players stranded. *Offensive Baseball Drills* puts you into scoring position. Now it's up to you to practice and take advantage of the opportunity to put more runs on the board.

KEY TO DIAGRAMS

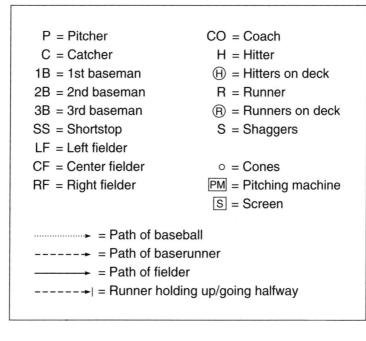

P = Pitcher	CO = Coach
C = Catcher	H = Hitter
1B = 1st baseman	Ⓗ = Hitters on deck
2B = 2nd baseman	R = Runner
3B = 3rd baseman	Ⓡ = Runners on deck
SS = Shortstop	S = Shaggers
LF = Left fielder	
CF = Center fielder	o = Cones
RF = Right fielder	PM = Pitching machine
	Ⓢ = Screen

⋯⋯⋯► = Path of baseball
− − − − − ► = Path of baserunner
———————► = Path of fielder
− − − − − ►| = Runner holding up/going halfway

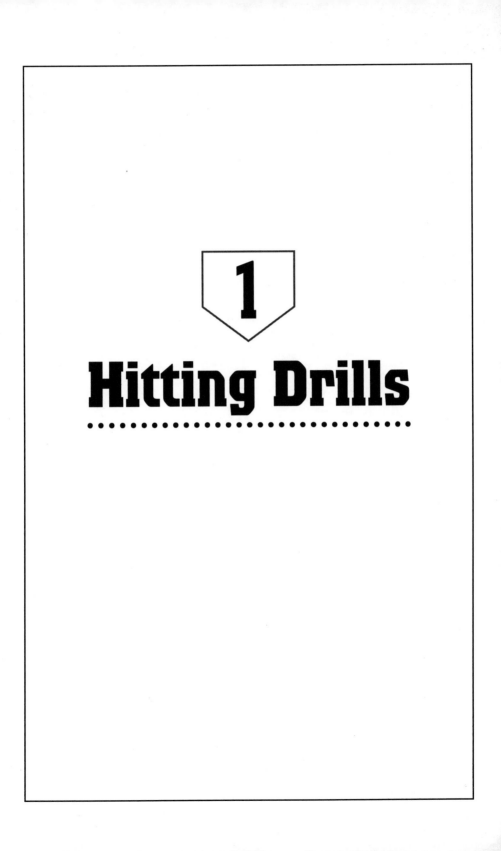

1

Hitting Drills

1
Hitting Drills

•••••••••••••••••••••••••

Hitting a baseball just might be the hardest skill to perform in all of sports. Where else are you considered a hero for having a 30 percent success rate?

Hitters must do many things right to make solid contact with a pitched baseball. And not just once, but consistently. In short, they must master the mechanics of hitting. The drills in this chapter will help players do just that. Through the practice of these 35 drills, players can develop and sharpen the hitting fundamentals that translate into consistent success at the plate. Specifically, the drills will help players

- track the ball;
- establish a "trigger action" with the hands;
- learn the proper hip rotation, shoulder and arm movement, and weight transfer;
- maintain body control and bat control;
- acquire or switch to a short, compact swing; and
- develop a proper follow-through.

In addition to these basic mechanics, good hitters know how to use the bat in any situation. When the team needs a line drive to the opposite field or a bunt to move a runner into scoring position, they can come through. Good hitters also know how to avoid committing too early to pitches, how to hit fastballs and curves, how to narrow their focus, and how to use an inside-out swing.

Yes, hitting *is* a very difficult skill. But it can be mastered, as Ted Williams, Joe DiMaggio, Hank Aaron, Tony Gwynn, and other great hitters have proven. And yet, even the best know there's always room for improvement. The drills that follow in this chapter will help players do just that.

1 One–Hand LAD Bat Drill

▌ Purpose

To develop the proper action of the lead arm in the swing

▌ Equipment

Batting cage or net, feeder or batting tee, short bat (LAD bat by Hit Rite)

▌ Procedure

1. Set up in an area that has a screened net or batting tunnel. You can do this drill in a garage, basement, yard, or gym.

2. Position yourself in front of a net or tunnel with a partner (feeder) kneeling about eight feet away, just off your front knee.

3. The feeder triggers the cocking action by dropping the throwing hand just before flipping the ball.

4. As the feeder flips the ball, cock your lead arm backward and swing with only the lead arm, using a short, quick downward swing.

▌ Key Points

- Younger players might want to choke up on the bat slightly.
- You can also use a tee with this drill if no one is available to flip the ball.
- Keep your front elbow from pointing up to the sky. Point it down to the ground as you complete your swing.
- Maintain sound fundamentals throughout your swing.

▌ Variation

The feeder can flip the ball inside, outside, and down the middle to work on different locations.

One–Hand LAD Bat Drill

No-Hitch Drill

▌ Purpose

To trigger the hands without dropping them below the shoulder

▌ Equipment

Cage area, bat, balls

▌ Procedure

1. Stand as usual in either the batter's box or batting cage.

2. Place the bat on your shoulder in a flat position.

3. When the coach throws the ball, lift the bat up and back off your shoulder and hit the ball.

▌ Key Points

- Keep your bat in a flat position—almost parallel to the ground. This will keep you from dropping your hands and "hitching" your swing.

- Lift the bat off your shoulder before you swing. Don't just swing from your back shoulder.

▌ Variation

This drill can also be used with the Tee Drill (#**12**) and the Soft-Toss Drill (#**16**).

No-Hitch Drill

Two-Hand LAD Bat Drill

∎ Purpose

To hit the ball on a line to the opposite field, emphasizing the use of the top hand

∎ Equipment

LAD bat, balls, chair, L-shaped screen

∎ Procedure

1. A feeder sits in a chair behind an L-shaped screen about 10 feet away from the plate.

2. A hitter stands at the plate in front of the screen, ready to hit.

3. The feeder throws the ball on the outside of the plate to the hitter.

4. The hitter hits the ball to the opposite field, emphasizing the use of the top hand.

5. The hitter takes 10 to 12 swings before a new hitter steps in.

∎ Key Points

- Take a short stride (six to eight inches) or even use the no-stride technique (#**9**) in this drill.

- Concentrate on hitting the top half of the ball with the bottom half of the bat.

- Hit the ball with both hands on the bat through the entire swing and follow-through.

Two-Hand LAD Bat Drill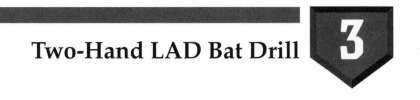

Diamond Demon

▮ Purpose

To develop the fundamentals of hitting using the Wiffle ball machine

▮ Equipment

Cage, Diamond Demon pitching machine, Wiffle balls, bats, home plate

▮ Procedure

1. Set up a hitting area with a home plate about 30 feet away from the Diamond Demon pitching machine. This drill can be set up in a batting cage or even an outfield grassy area.

2. A coach or player stands behind the machine with a bucket of Wiffle balls, ready to feed the machine.

3. As the machine pitches, the hitter practices the fundamentals of hitting.

▮ Key Points

- This is a relatively safe drill, so it doesn't *require* a batting cage. But the hitter shouldn't get too close, even though the feeder can control the speed of the machine. And the feeder should stand far enough from the hitter to avoid being hit by a ball.

- After each pitch, the feeder should give the hitter time to get ready for the next pitch.

▮ Variation

Set up the Diamond Demon to throw to the outside corner so the hitter can hit to the opposite field.

Diamond Demon

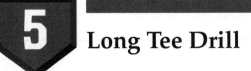

Long Tee Drill

▌ Purpose

To learn how to drive through the ball, and consistently hit line drives. By hitting off the tee three to four feet from the net you don't always get a clear picture of how to hit the ball. With this drill, players learn how to consistently hit line drives.

▌ Equipment

Batting tee, bat, balls, batting tunnel

▌ Procedure

1. Set a ball on a tee about 30 feet in front of the net (not shown in photo).

2. Place a home plate behind the tee so you can adjust your stance in relation to the plate.

3. Hit line drives into the back of the net.

▌ Key Points

- Pair up with another player; one feeds (sets the ball on the tee) and the other hits.

- Try to hit line drives that will carry to the back wall of the batting tunnel.

- Adjust the tee to different heights to practice hitting low and high pitches.

- If you hit under the ball, you will hit the top of the net toward the back of the tunnel.

- If you hit on top of the ball, you will hit a ground ball 15 to 20 feet from the tee.

Long Tee Drill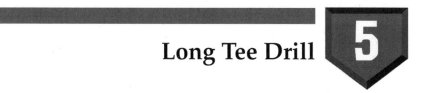

Pivot-Rotation

∎ Purpose

To develop proper hip rotation while pivoting on your back foot and remaining balanced

∎ Equipment

Bat, fungo, or stick

∎ Procedure

1. Put your bat behind your back and lock your arms around the bat.

2. Assume your normal stance and pop your hips quickly, rotating your trunk while pivoting on your back foot.

3. After you rotate, remain balanced and don't move either foot.

∎ Key Points

- Rotate on the ball of your back foot.
- Your belly button should be pointing toward the pitcher after you rotate.
- By learning proper hip rotation and thrust, you'll learn how to generate power and bat speed.

Pivot-Rotation

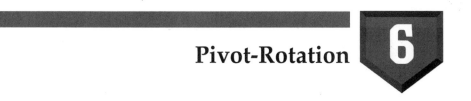

7 Bunting for a Hit

▌ Purpose

To learn how to bunt for a base hit

▌ Equipment

Balls, bats, pitching machine, cones

▌ Procedure

1. Have a pitcher throw from the mound or set up a pitching machine in front of the pitcher's mound.

2. Position infielders (or shaggers) in the field and a catcher at home plate.

3. Set up cones to designate areas for hitters to drop their bunts in.

4. The hitter assumes a normal stance and shows bunt after the ball has been thrown.

5. The hitter takes one crossover step toward first base after bunting the ball.

▌ Key Points

- Don't show bunt until the ball has been thrown.
- Bunt the ball in the designated areas and count the number of balls that go between the cones successfully.
- Bunt the ball before starting the crossover toward first base.
- Placement is more important than the jump out of the box.
- Set the proper bat angle to place the ball in the correct spot on the field.

Bunting for a Hit

8 Bunting Technique

▎ Purpose

To develop the technique and bat control used for sacrifice and safety bunts

▎ Equipment

Baseballs, bats, cones

▎ Procedure

1. Mark off two lines five to ten feet away from home plate. Cones or balls can also be used to mark off a certain area.

2. Set up a pitcher and catcher, and one player on each of the base lines (shaggers) to retrieve bunted balls.

3. Get in the bunting stance before the pitcher releases the ball.

4. Work on the techniques of the sacrifice bunt, trying to bunt the ball into the designated areas.

5. Each player bunts the ball to both sides several times.

▎ Key Points

- The pitcher's velocity should simulate a game condition.
- Angle the barrel of the bat upward at a 45° angle.
- Extend your arms and flex your legs to bunt low and high pitches.
- Work on getting the ball to stop in the designated areas by deadening the ball with the proper technique.
- Don't run out of the box toward first base too soon. When sacrificing, bunt the ball, see it hit the ground, and then run.

Bunting Technique

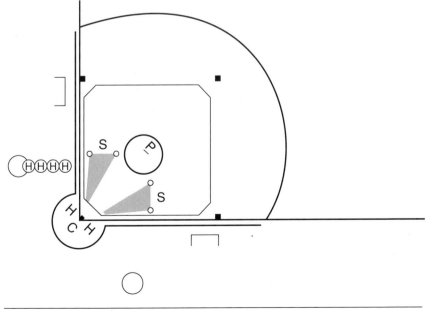

No-Stride Drill

▌ Purpose

To focus on the use of the hands in hitting

▌ Equipment

Bat, shape screen or batting cage, balls

Procedure

1. Stand with your feet spread more than shoulder-width apart, about one to two feet wider than normal.
2. A coach or player flips a ball from a short-toss station.
3. Cock your bat and swing, pivoting on your back foot. With your feet widely spread, you don't need to stride.
4. Remain balanced after your swing.

Key Points

- Don't take a stride. Isolate your upper body and develop a short, deliberate trigger action with your hands.
- Maintain proper mechanics for the entire swing—watch the ball, rotate your hips, swing downward, and follow through.

No-Stride Drill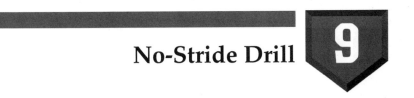

Two-Hand Toss

∎ Purpose

To develop a cocking (trigger) action with the hands, a pivoting action with the back foot, and a short swing. This drill helps develop quick hands and a short stride.

∎ Equipment

Fence or 5' × 5' net and balls (Incrediballs by Easton can also be used)

∎ Procedure

1. Get in your batting stance with a ball in each hand (top photo).
2. Cock both hands to trigger the swing (bottom photo).
3. With a short, quick swinging action, release the balls into the net at the end of your swing.

∎ Key Points

- The trigger should be short and slow instead of long and quick.
- Pivot on your back foot and remain balanced, using a compact swing.
- As you release the balls, the hand action should come inside and then out.

Two-Hand Toss

Inside-Out Swing Drill

▌ Purpose

To develop a short, quick, inside-out swing that takes the bat directly to the ball

Equipment

Bat and net (or a wall)

▌ Procedure

1. Place the knob of the bat against your stomach with the top of the bat touching the net or wall.
2. Get in your hitting stance.
3. Take an inside-out swing, with the end of the bat just barely scraping the net or wall. If you can, use a net rather than a wall to avoid damaging the bat (or the wall).

▌ Key Points

- Don't pull your front shoulder away from the wall to adjust the arch of the swing.
- If you swing with your arms, you will create a long, looping swing, hitting the net and keeping you from finishing your swing.
- The hands should come in front of the chest and then extend outward.
- This is a great drill to do while on deck waiting to hit.

Inside-Out Swing Drill

Tee Drill

▌ Purpose

To develop a smooth, compact swing

▌ Equipment

Net or cage, batting tee, bat, balls

▌ Procedure

1. Pair up players so that one (the feeder) places the ball on the tee while the other hits.

2. Place a batting tee in front of home plate. (You can purchase a tee or make one out of radiator hose, pipes, and a wooden base.)

3. The hitter takes a normal stance at home plate.

4. Move the tee to different areas in front of the plate to help hitters practice hitting inside, middle, and outside pitches.

5. Raise the tee to different heights to give hitters practice hitting high and low pitches.

▌ Key Points

- Allow the feeder to get in a safe position, away from the tee, before swinging.

- Younger players may use tennis balls or Incrediballs for safety purposes.

- After hitting the ball, check to see that the body remained balanced and the pivot was made on the back foot.

Tee Drill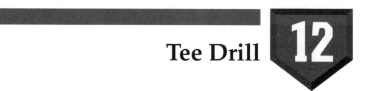

Trigger-Stride Drill

▌ Purpose

To learn weight transfer, body control, timing, and to groove a compact swing

▌ Equipment

Batting tunnel or a 5' × 5' net, bat, balls

▌ Procedure

1. Set up in an area that has a screened net or a batting tunnel, like a garage, basement, or yard.

2. Set up in a hitting stance in front of the net or tunnel, with a partner kneeling about 10 feet away, just off your front knee.

3. The feeder triggers your cocking action by dropping his hand just before flipping the ball.

4. Time a short, compact swing, hitting the ball to the appropriate field, depending on where the feeder flips it.

▌ Key Points

- The feeder should float the ball, not throw it on a line.
- If the feeder flips the ball inside, turn on the ball and drive it to the left of the net, simulating a hit to left field (for a right-handed hitter).
- If the feeder flips the ball over the middle of the plate, drive it back up the middle.
- If the feeder flips the ball outside, drive the ball to the right side of the net, simulating a hit to right field (for a right-handed hitter).
- The feeder should allow the hitter to get set between tosses.
- Freeze the action after contact to check your balance and follow-through.

Trigger-Stride Drill

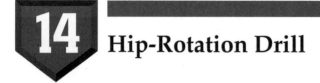

Hip-Rotation Drill

▮ Purpose

To develop proper hip rotation and learn how to remain balanced at the point of contact, skills necessary to pull the baseball

▮ Equipment

Batting cage, 5' x 5' net, bat, balls (Incrediballs or tennis balls are recommended)

▮ Procedure

1. Set up in front of a net or at the plate with a feeder kneeling in front of you, just off your front hip.

2. The feeder flips the ball toward your front hip so that you can pivot and drive the ball into the net to the left (for a right-handed hitter). Use a batting tee if you don't have someone to feed you pitches.

3. The feeder should alternate high and low tosses to help you learn how to adjust your hands to different pitches.

▮ Key Points

- Keep your front foot closed.
- Don't hit the ball back at the feeder. Using Incrediballs or tennis balls is highly recommended.
- Concentrate on a short, quick swing while pivoting on your back foot and turning the toe of your shoe toward the pitcher.
- Watch for balance in the stance, balance in the swing, and driving the ball to left field (right-handed hitter).
- Remain balanced and don't allow the front foot to move left or right after contact.

Hip-Rotation Drill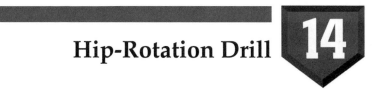

Hitting Fungoes

▌ Purpose

To develop proper hand action, weight shift, downward swing, and follow-through

▌ Equipment

Fungo and balls

▌ Procedure

1. Players who are waiting on deck hit fungoes to the fielders on their side of the infield.

2. Include up to four hitters in each of three hitting stations. Hitters rotate to the back of the line of another hitting station after taking a certain number of swings. After a complete rotation of the hitters through all three hitting stations, one line can rotate to the infield spots and the infielders can come in to bat.

3. Concentrate on hitting the top half of the baseball with a short, downward swing.

▌ Key Points

- Maintain balance throughout the entire swing.
- Use a short, quick stroke to hit the ball.
- Don't transfer too much weight forward when you contact the baseball.

Hitting Fungoes

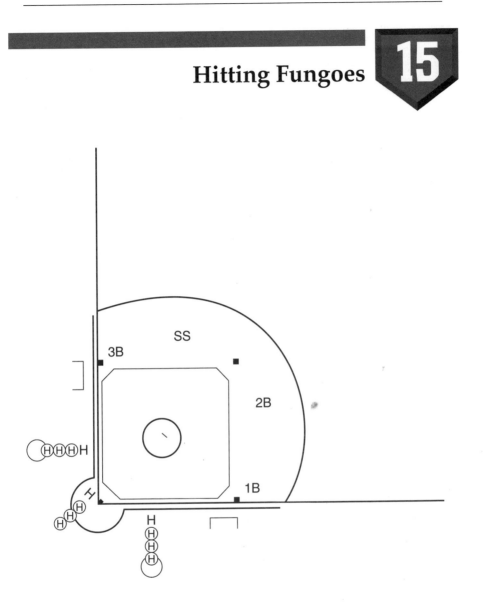

Soft-Toss Drill

▌ Purpose

To learn how to trigger, strike, and swing

▌ Equipment

Cage, soft toss machine (by ATEC), baseballs, flip net

▌ Procedure

1. Position the machine at a 45° angle so the ball flips at your front hip.
2. Drive the ball back up the middle.
3. Use a buddy system: Hit 12 balls and then switch positions.
4. Alter the machine's position to practice hitting both inside and outside pitches.

▌ Key Points

- Maintain balance and fundamentals throughout your swing.
- Execute proper weight shift and timing to hit the ball consistently.

Soft-Toss Drill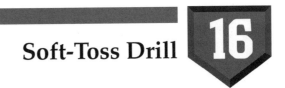

Tracking the Baseball

▌ Purpose

To focus on the baseball and visually track the ball from the mound to the plate

▌ Equipment

Bullpen area, cage (short toss), baseballs, bat, helmet

▌ Procedure

1. Assume your stance at the plate and trigger.
2. Look in the area where the pitcher is going to release the ball.
3. Stride and focus on the ball coming out of the pitcher's hand.
4. Watch the ball all the way into the catcher's mitt or net.

▌ Key Point

- Do this drill in the cage during short toss or in the bullpen during station work.
- Don't just focus on seeing the ball—narrow your focus to look for the ball's seams.
- As you trigger-stride, keep about 70 percent of your weight on the back foot while tracking the ball.

Tracking the Baseball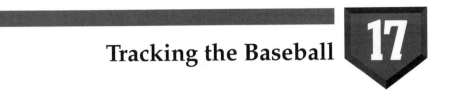

Bounce Drill

▌ Purpose

To develop weight shift, hand-eye coordination, and timing

▌ Equipment

Flip net, cage, cement block, bat, baseballs

▌ Procedure

1. Set up in front of a net with a feeder kneeling about 10 feet away, just off your front knee.

2. The feeder triggers your cocking action by bouncing the ball off the cement block or ground at a 45° angle so it bounces up for a strike in front of the plate.

3. If the ball bounces inside, turn on the ball and drive it to the left of the net, simulating a hit to left field (for a right-handed hitter).

4. If the ball bounces in the middle, hit it back up the middle.

5. If the ball bounces to the outside, drive the ball to the right of the net, simulating a hit to right field (for a right-handed hitter).

▌ Key Points

- A curveball can be simulated by bouncing the ball above the waist and having the hitter hit the ball on the way down.

- The feeder should allow the hitter to get set between pitches.

Bounce Drill

One-Knee Drill

▎ Purpose

To isolate the upper body and concentrate on a short, quick, compact swing

▎ Equipment

Batting tee or feeder, cage or flip net, balls

▎ Procedure

1. Place the batting tee directly in front of the plate in order to hit the ball back up the middle.

2. Take your stance next to the tee with your back knee on the ground and your front leg extended slightly.

3. Adjust the tee so you hit the ball just above the belt area.

4. Trigger and swing, driving the ball into the net.

▎ Key Points

- Use your hands to swing the bat instead of hitting with your shoulders.

- Avoid the tendency to swing up at the ball. Hit the top half of the ball with the bottom half of the bat.

- Hit through the ball as if you were swinging at three balls lined up one right after the other.

One-Knee Drill

One-Knee Drill With Feeder

Opposite-Field Hitting

▋ Purpose

To learn to wait on the ball and hit the outside pitch to the opposite field

▋ Equipment

L-shaped screen, field, baseballs, bats, batting cage, batting helmets (you can also use a pitching machine)

▋ Procedure

1. Set up the L-shaped screen on the right side of the pitching mound as viewed from the right-handed hitter, and on the left side for a left-handed hitter.
2. Players break up into two groups: left-handed and right-handed hitters.
3. Throw batting practice from either the left or right side of the pitching mound.
4. Shaggers take all positions on the field.
5. The hitter looks for a pitch away and hits the ball back in the direction it came from.

▋ Key Points

- Don't alter your stance regardless of the direction the pitch is coming from.
- Look for a pitch on the outer half of the plate and drive the ball back at the screen.
- Hit line drives or ground balls.

Opposite-Field Hitting

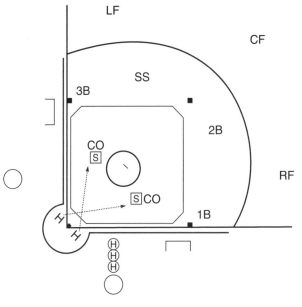

Weight-Shift Drill

∎ Purpose

To develop proper stride technique while maintaining correct weight shift

∎ Equipment

Bat and mirror (if available)

∎ Procedure

1. Assume your normal stance with a bat. If a mirror is available, use it to check your technique.

2. Cock your bat and stride forward, keeping your weight back and striding with your front foot. Cock your hands backward as your foot goes forward six to eight inches.

3. Stride on the inside of your front foot, picking the heel up slightly off the ground.

∎ Key Points

- Do this drill repeatedly to develop a good habit of proper weight transfer in the trigger and stride.

- Practice this drill while on deck waiting to hit in a game or practice.

Weight-Shift Drill

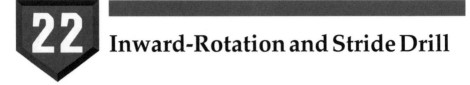

Inward-Rotation and Stride Drill

▋ Purpose

To practice inward rotation of the front side, stride, and weight transfer, helping the hitter develop essential timing and rhythm

▋ Equipment

Batting tunnel or cage, balls, bat, screen

▋ Procedure

1. Assume a perpendicular position at the plate as the pitcher (not shown in photo) stands 40 to 50 feet away behind a screen.

2. As the pitcher starts to release the ball, rotate inward toward the catcher with your lead shoulder pointing at the pitcher.

3. Swing and hit the ball, using proper mechanics.

▋ Key Points

- This drill is especially designed for the hitter who has no trigger, or inward rotation of the knee, shoulder, and front side.

- Maintain a weight transfer of 60 percent back and 40 percent forward after taking a stride.

- The pitcher should throw from a short distance (40 to 50 feet) to maintain accuracy.

Inward-Rotation and Stride Drill

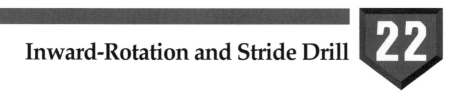

Pepper Game

▌ Purpose

To develop bat control and a short, quick swing

▌ Equipment

Baseballs and bat

▌ Procedure

1. Stand approximately 22 feet away from the three fielders, who position themselves two feet apart.
2. Hit the ball using a short, quick, downward stroke.
3. Hit the ball sharply with one or two hops (ground balls) to the fielders.
4. A fielder fields the ball and quickly tosses a half to three-quarter speed pitch back to be hit.
5. Hit the ball where it is pitched.
6. Preferably use four players in this drill and not more than five.

▌ Key Points

- Hit the inside pitch to the fielder to your left (for a right-handed batter).
- Hit the pitch in the middle to the fielder directly in front of you.
- Hit the outside pitch to the fielder to your right (for a right-handed batter).
- To make the drill more difficult, use two baseballs at once, keeping the hitter constantly ready to swing and fielders always heads-up.

Pepper Game

24 Short-Toss Station Drill

▌ Purpose

To develop the proper hitting mechanics and learn to hit to the opposite field

▌ Equipment

L-shaped screen, batting tunnel, bat, balls

▌ Procedure

1. Set up the screen approximately 40 feet away from home plate.
2. Pitches should be thrown to the inside, outside, and middle of the plate.
3. Drive the ball into right field (for a right-handed hitter) or left field (for a left-handed hitter).

▌ Key Points

- Because of the short throwing distance, this drill allows the coach to throw more strikes, giving each player more reps.
- This drill can be performed on the diamond as well as in the batting tunnel.

Short-Toss Station Drill

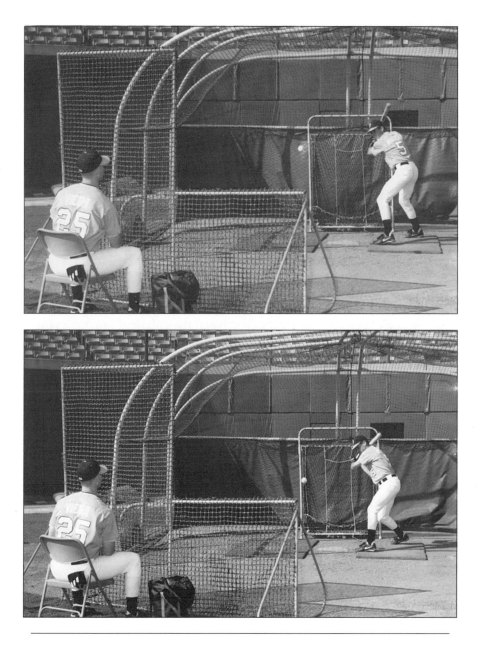

Hit-by-Pitch Drill

▌ Purpose

To develop the proper technique to get hit by a pitch

▌ Equipment

Tennis balls or Incrediballs and helmet

▌ Procedure

1. Take your stance at the plate or in front of a cage or net.

2. A coach or player throws balls at you and to the inside.

3. Turn in toward the catcher, allowing the ball to hit you in the back. This will protect the front of your body and ease the impact of the ball.

▌ Key Points

• Never use real baseballs, only tennis balls or Incrediballs.

• Tuck your chin in and back toward the catcher to protect your face.

• Tuck your front elbow into your side to prevent being hit in the elbow.

Hit-by-Pitch Drill

Hit-Stick Drill

▌ Purpose

To narrow your focus while grooving your swing

▌ Equipment

Broomstick or hit stick (by Easton), plastic golf balls or baseballs, cage or flip net

▌ Procedure

1. A feeder kneels about 10 feet away, just off your front knee.

2. The feeder triggers your cocking action by dropping his hand just before flipping the plastic golf ball.

3. Hit the ball with a broomstick or hit stick, driving the ball into the net.

▌ Key Points

• At first, make a smooth swing at about 90 percent normal bat speed to be sure to make contact.

• Concentrate on hitting the ball squarely.

• Maintain good balance, weight shift, hand action, and a sound finish.

Hit-Stick Drill

Hit-Rite Quick or Die Drill

▌ Purpose

To learn how to adjust to fastballs and curveballs

▌ Equipment

Hit-Rite machine and bat

▌ Procedure

1. Stand in a normal stance ready to hit.
2. Trigger your hands before you swing.
3. Make contact with the ball.

▌ Key Points

- The feeder should hold the cable assembly while standing between the net and height adjustment far enough back to avoid being hit by the ball after contact.
- The feeder should vary the pitches, using fastballs, changes, and curveballs.
- To throw a breaking pitch, the feeder should hold the cable assembly chest high and flip the ball out of the hand toward the right.
- To throw a normal fastball, the feeder should hold the cable assembly about chin high and release.
- To increase the speed of a fastball, the feeder should raise the cable assembly higher and release.

Hit-Rite Quick or Die Drill

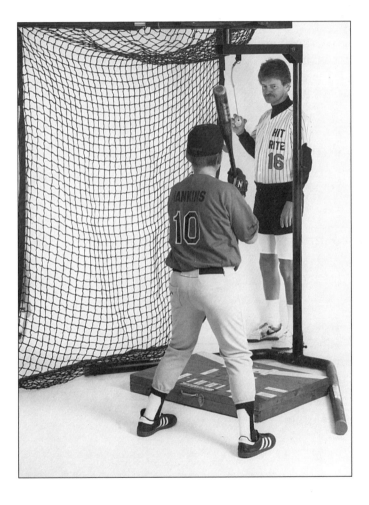

Hit-Rite Off-Speed Drill

▌ Purpose

To learn to keep your hands back and not commit too early on off-speed pitches

▌ Equipment

Bat, Hit-Rite machine, net

▌ Procedure

1. Take your normal position behind the Hit-Rite machine.
2. A coach stands facing you and to your back at a 45° angle from your back foot while holding the cable assembly chin high.
3. Look toward the netting while being able to peripherally see the coach's movement.
4. Stride when you see movement but keep your hands back.
5. Make contact before the ball hits the net.

▌ Key Points

- The feeder should simulate both right- and left-handed curveballs.
- The feeder should simulate a faster fastball by holding the ball higher.

Hit-Rite Off-Speed Drill

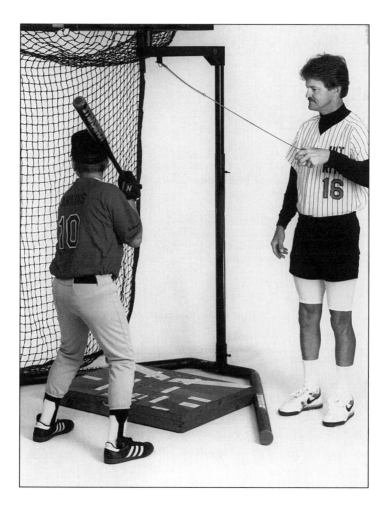

Swing King

▌ Purpose

To learn how to swing down and through the ball with a good punch

▌ Equipment

Swing King and bat

▌ Procedure

1. Position yourself behind the Swing King to hit a ball back up the middle.

2. Take a short, quick swing with a consistent follow-through.

3. Drive the bat through the plane of the ball, maintaining sound hitting fundamentals.

▌ Key Points

- The Swing King can be adjusted for right- and left-handed hitters.

- As you make contact, envision driving through the ball as if you were hitting three balls in a row.

- If you make contact and drive through the ball, the Swing King will spin around without bouncing. If you don't, the arm will bounce as it pivots around its base.

- If you hit the ball correctly, you will produce a ground ball, line drive stroke.

Swing King

Swing Trainer Drill

▌ Purpose

To develop a consistent swing and eliminate pulling the shoulder, lifting the front arm, or pulling your head off the ball

▌ Equipment

Bat and Swing Trainer

▌ Procedure

1. Set up a hitting area in your basement, cage area, or garage.
2. Stand behind the wheels of the Swing Trainer to simulate hitting a ball in front of the plate.
3. Swing at the pitches, concentrating on keeping your head steady and not pulling your shoulder or lifting your arm.

▌ Key Points

- Keep your head steady.
- The machine can be adjusted for right- and left-handed batters.
- You can develop your hands and forearms by choosing the gap between the lines.
- You will also develop strong wrists and forearms—a must for good hitting.
- This drill will also teach you to go through the ball and develop a strong follow-through.

▌ Variations

Adjust the machine for different types of swings—down, level, up, opposite field, foul, and so forth.

Swing Trainer Drill

Solar Hitter

▌ Purpose

To develop a consistent, grooved swing with proper hitting mechanics

▌ Equipment

Solar Hitter and bat

▌ Procedure

1. The coach stands beside the Solar Hitter (optional).

2. Prepare for either an inside, middle, or outside pitch.

3. Hit the ball using sound fundamentals with a consistent follow-through.

▌ Key Points

- Adjust the ball for inside, outside, high, and low pitch locations, not just down the middle.

- Take about 25 to 30 swings and then go to another zone or height.

Solar Hitter

Towel Bat Drill

▌ Purpose

To develop a quick inside-out swing

▌ Equipment

Wooden bat and eye bolt-towel and tie

▌ Procedure

1. Assume your normal stance.

2. On a given command or on your own, trigger, stride, and swing, causing the towel to make a popping sound.

3. Finish your swing with the proper mechanics.

▌ Key Points

- Swing the towel bat with your hands, not your arms.
- Snap your wrists to make the towel pop.

Towel Bat Drill

Double-Tee Inside-Out Swing Drill

▌ Purpose

To develop an inside-out swing

▌ Equipment

Double tee, bat, baseballs, cage area

▌ Procedure

1. Place the double tee in a cage area. Position one stand for an inside pitch, the other for an outside pitch.
2. Place a ball on both stands.
3. Take your stance in the cage near the double tee.
4. Hit the inside pitch first, then the outside pitch.

▌ Key Points

- Use an inside-out swing to hit both inside and outside pitches.
- If you use an outside-in swing or a long swing, you'll hit both baseballs off the tees.

▌ Variation

A coach or teammate can direct you to react and hit either the inside or outside pitch.

Double-Tee Inside-Out Swing Drill

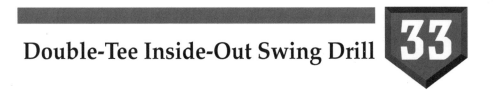

Double-Tee Swing-Down Drill

▍ Purpose

To develop a short, downward swing and avoid an upper-cut swing

▍ Equipment

Double tee, bat, baseballs, cage area

▍ Procedure

1. Position the stands right behind each other on the double tee and place a baseball on each.

2. Take your stance beside the double tee, ready to hit a ball back up the middle.

3. Trigger, stride, swing, and hit the baseball in front, avoiding the ball behind it.

▍ Key Points

• Swing downward and avoid an upper-cut swing. If you upper-cut, you'll hit the back baseball.

Double-Tee Swing-Down Drill

Swing Hit Trainer

▍Purpose

To teach the hitter to groove a consistent swing at different locations

▍Equipment

Swing Hit Trainer and bat

▍Procedure

1. One player grabs a bat and takes a hitting position.
2. Another player holds the extended Swing Hit Trainer and stands about eight to ten feet away from the hitter.
3. The holder positions the trainer so that it is about two feet in front of the hitter's front hip.
4. The hitter triggers, strides, and swings, hitting the trainer.
5. After the third step out of the batter's box, the hitter should glance toward the coach. If the coach is holding up one arm, the runner runs through the base.
6. The holder and hitter switch positions.

▍Key Points

- After the follow-through, the hitter checks to see if he maintained proper balance, pivoted on the back foot, and kept the head down.
- Work on inside, outside, middle, high, and low pitches.
- The holder can move the trainer around to work on different pitch locations.

▍Variation

Hitters can work on the high pitch while kneeling on the back leg with the other leg extended. This isolates the upper body.

Swing Hit Trainer

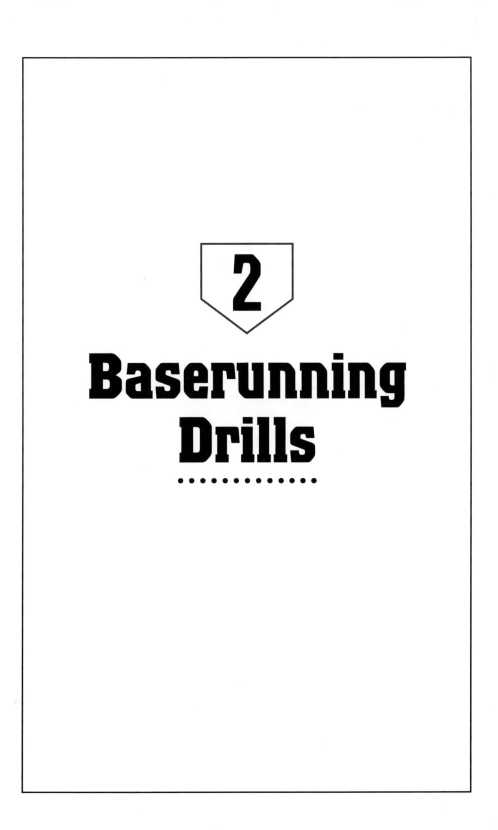

2

Baserunning Drills

2
Baserunning Drills

· ·

Even good hitters have slumps. They might be hitting line drives, but right at the defense. Or they could just be facing a series of tough, overpowering pitchers. Whatever the case, you can't always count on the bats to produce. That's why baserunning skills are so important.

As they say, speed doesn't slump! Without question, speed is a great asset in baseball. But baserunning involves much more than speed. Unless you know when and how to use it, speed may mean you just run yourself into a lot of outs. Good baserunners know when to take the extra base, how to read outfielders, which balls are going in the gaps, which slide to use to avoid the tag, how to read the pitcher and get a good jump, how to execute the cross-over step, and so on.

Smart baserunning is one of the most exciting and effective offensive weapons you can employ. You can generate runs on the base paths with minimal hitting. And alert, aggressive baserunning puts more pressure on the defense. One mental lapse or lazy throw means an extra base. And many opposing pitchers become rattled by crafty baserunners. Not only do they expend energy holding runners to short leadoffs, they also lose concentration on the hitter because of their concern about the runners.

Maury Wills, Lou Brock, and Rickey Henderson are just a few of the players who used their superb baserunning skills to great advantage throughout their careers. The 20 drills in this chapter will help players learn, practice, and master the baserunning skills and plays that are part of any complete offensive package.

36 Reading Pitchers' Moves

▋ Purpose

To develop visual concentration on a certain body part or idiosyncrasy of a pitcher

▋ Equipment

Grassy area in the outfield or first base area of the infield

▋ Procedure

1. Players align in three lines of four and the lead players get into a stealing lead.

2. Runners watch for a certain move (for example, head or shoulder movement) from the pitcher.

3. The pitcher demonstrates certain pickoff moves and then throws to the plate so the baserunners can practice in game-like conditions.

4. The players shout as soon as they see the move and return to their "base" as they read the move.

▋ Key Points

• Players should concentrate on reading just the pitcher's move.

• Players should focus on a specific move. If stealing off the shoulder, they shouldn't look at the whole body, but concentrate on the shoulder.

Reading Pitchers' Moves

Getting a Jump

▮ Purpose

To learn how to read a pitcher's move and get a good jump

▮ Equipment

Grassy area in the outfield or first base area of the infield

▮ Procedure

1. Players align in three lines of four and get into a stealing lead.

2. From the mound, the coach tells the players to watch for a certain move; the pitcher then demonstrates that move.

3. The pitcher gets into a stretch position.

4. The players yell "back" or "go" after they take the crossover step toward second.

5. Focus on the pitcher's movement and then break toward second in a straight line.

▮ Key Points

• Move as soon as the pitcher moves—get a great jump.

• Take only a couple of steps in either direction at first. Later go all the way back to first or all the way to second.

• As you cross over, make sure you stay low and don't stand up to run.

Getting a Jump

Reaction Drill

▌ Purpose

To learn awareness and proper mechanics when running from home plate to first base

▌ Equipment

Infield and bat

▌ Procedure

1. A player stands at home plate, bat in hand. Other players line up behind him.

2. A coach is in the infield grass between third base and short-stop.

3. The player swings, crosses over out of the box, and heads down the line toward first base.

4. On his third step, he glances at the coach. If the coach is holding up one arm, the player runs through the base. If the coach is holding up two arms, he veers out because the ball went through the infield.

▌ Key Points

- Alternate signals to keep the runners honest.
- Players should not run before swinging the bat.
- Players should *glance*—not stare—at the coach.
- Some players will need to veer out more than others when making a turn.
- Players should not slow down before getting to the bag; they should run through the base.

Reaction Drill

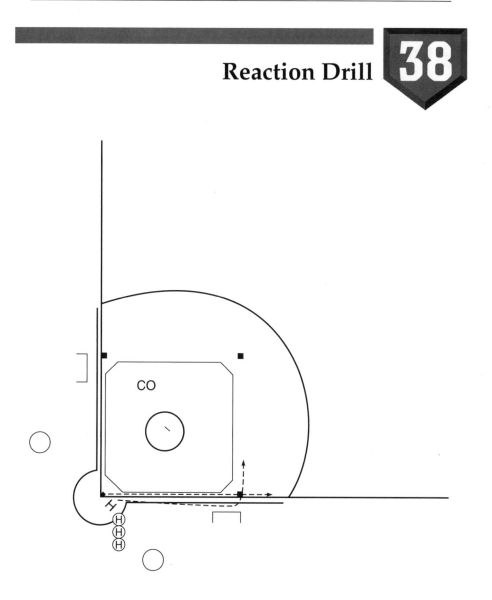

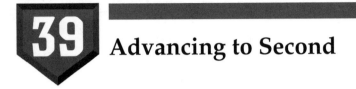

Advancing to Second

▮ Purpose

To learn how to take the extra base

▮ Equipment

Baseball field, fungo, baseballs, helmets

▮ Procedure

1. Players with helmets on line up at home.

2. Nine players with warm, loose arms take the field. (You can also use just outfielders.)

3. A coach stands at home with a fungo bat and plenty of baseballs.

4. As the coach hits the ball into the outfield on the ground, a player runs to first, rounds the bag, and reads the outfielder. The runner can stay at first or try to advance to second.

▮ Key Points

- A coach in the outfield can make sure the outfielders don't break in too early.

- Outfielders can also work on their defensive skills.

- Runners should run hard between home and first, anticipating going to second base.

- Runners should work on learning which hits they can take the extra base on.

- As a variation, use base coaches.

Advancing to Second 39

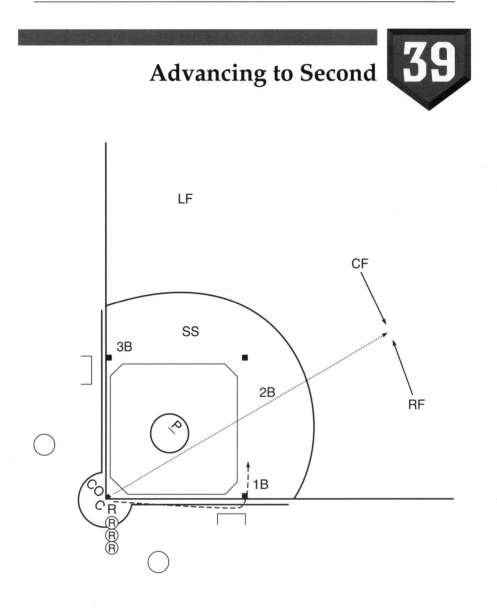

Advancing From First to Third

▌ Purpose

To know when to advance from first to third on a hit

▌ Equipment

Fungo bat, baseballs, helmets, baseball field

▌ Procedure

1. Line up several players wearing batting helmets at first base and home plate.

2. Position a full team in the field, or use just outfielders and a catcher. Make sure arms are loose.

3. A coach is at home plate with a fungo bat and plenty of baseballs.

4. As the coach grounds the ball into the outfield, the runner on first heads to second base and the player at home heads to first base. They read the outfielder to determine whether they can advance an extra base.

▌ Key Points

• Runners must read the ball to determine whether they can advance.

• Outfielders can work on their defensive skills.

• The runner at home should not force the other runner to go to third by "running him off" second.

• For a variation, use base coaches.

Advancing From First to Third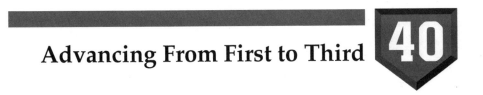

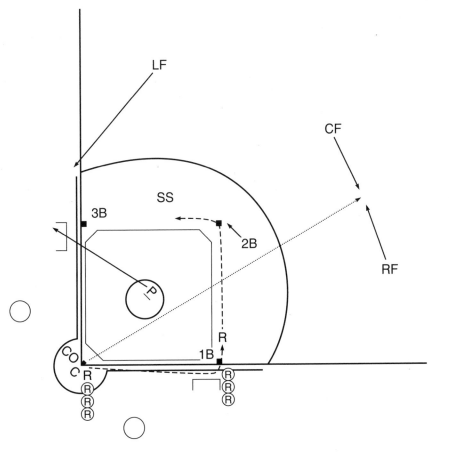

Crossover Drill

▌ Purpose

To learn how to cross over and pivot on the right foot

▌ Equipment

Grassy area in right field, outfield foul lines, batting gloves

▌ Procedure

1. The players pair up. One player (stealer) is in a stealing position and the other (partner) stands in front of him, just off his right foot.

2. The partner holds a batting glove in front of himself, about waist high.

3. The stealer reaches with his left arm to grab the glove and then crosses over.

4. As he grabs the glove, he crosses over with his left foot and pulls his left arm back in sync. The grab-and-crossover action puts the arms and legs in sync on the first step, developing the quickness needed to steal a base.

▌ Key Points

- The first move should be a sudden burst of energy.
- Snatch the glove quickly with your left hand.
- As you cross over, keep in a straight line with second base.

Crossover Drill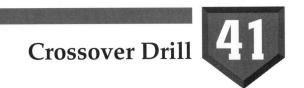

Reads in the Outfield

▮ Purpose

To teach runners on first base to read the balls that are in the gap or over the outfielders' heads

▮ Equipment

Baseballs, fungo, field, helmets

▮ Procedure

1. Line up runners at first base wearing batting helmets.
2. Position players in all positions.
3. Position a coach just in front of the mound in the grassy area.
4. The first runner takes his primary lead off first base, and, as the coach throws the ball up to hit, moves out to his secondary lead.
5. The runner reacts to the hit and advances as far as he can.

▮ Key Points

- Hit balls that the outfielders can catch or that are barely out of their reach while sprinting for the ball.
- If, on a catchable fly ball, the runner sees the outfielder's number on his back, he should go as far as he can toward second.
- On a fly ball hit to deep left field, the runner may go all the way to second and even round the bag and take a couple of steps toward third.
- Runners need to go 100 percent, as in a game. If they can make third or home on a hit over the outfielder's head, great!
- You may elect to use a third base coach to help the runners.

Reads in the Outfield 42

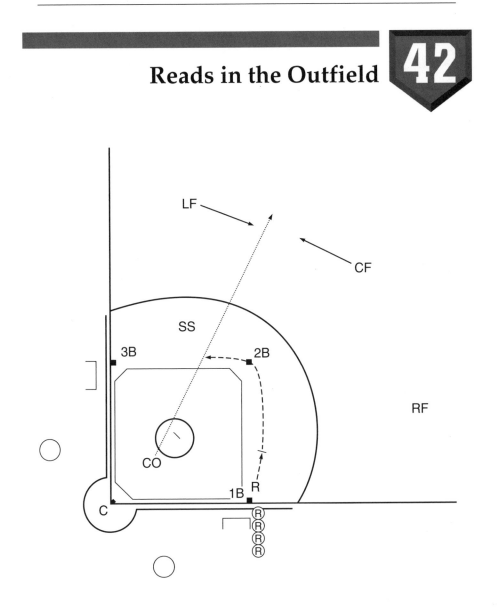

First-and-Third Steal Drill: LHP

▮ Purpose

To learn how to execute a double steal with a left-handed pitcher

▮ Equipment

Infield, bases, indoor facility or gym.

▮ Procedure

1. Split your baserunners into two groups: infielders at first base, outfielders at third base. Players form lines at each base.

2. A left-handed coach or pitcher is on the mound, and a catcher and first baseman are in place.

3. When the pitcher is set and the runner at first draws eye contact, this runner extends his lead, enticing the pitcher to try to pick him off.

4. Both runners break on the first movement of the pitcher.

5. If the pitcher throws to first, the runner at third breaks for the plate.

6. If the pitcher throws to the plate, the runner at third returns to third, while the runner at first steals second.

7. Run the drill for three minutes and then rotate infielders and outfielders.

▮ Key Points

- The runner at first doesn't extend his lead until he draws eye contact, after the pitcher is set.

- The runner at first should never lose eye contact with the pitcher.

- The runner at third must make sure that the pitcher is throwing to first before breaking for home.

- In a game, the hitter must take the pitch no matter what happens.

First-and-Third Steal Drill: LHP **43**

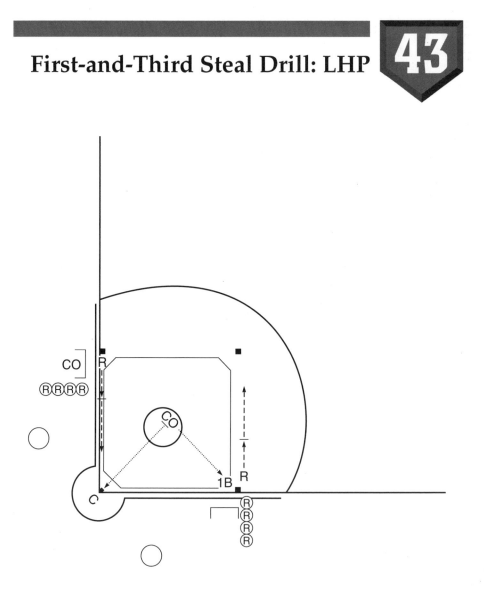

Three Stops Drill

▌ Purpose

To learn how to run the bases effectively, especially when one or more bases are occupied

▌ Equipment

Infield, bases, indoor facility or gym

▌ Procedure

1. Divide your team into three groups and place them in lines at home, first, and second.
2. Position your third base coach in the third base coaching box.
3. With a command from the third base coach, the three baserunners begin running simultaneously.
4. The coach can either stop the lead runner at third or let him score.
5. On the next play, the coach can allow the runner to score from first or stop the runner at second with a double. The options are endless.
6. Perform this drill for four to six minutes nonstop.

▌ Key Points

- Run hard with your head up.
- Run aggressively and smart.
- Be aware of the player in front of you.

Three Stops Drill 44

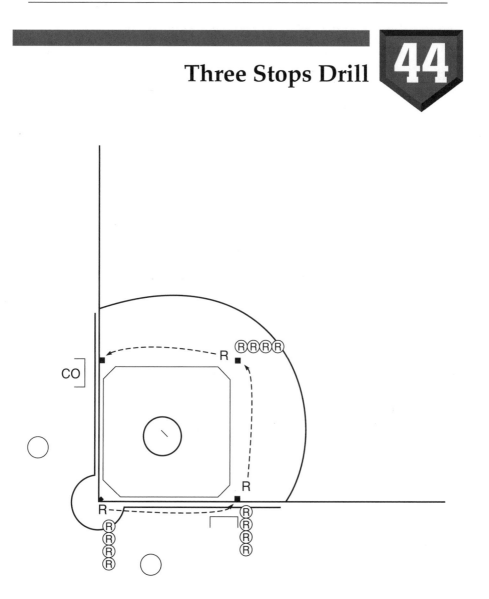

First-and-Third Steal Drill: RHP

▌ Purpose

To learn how to execute a double steal on a right-handed pitcher

▌ Equipment

Infield, bases, indoor facility or gym

▌ Procedure

1. Divide your players into two groups: outfielders at first base, infielders at third base. Players form lines at each base.
2. Place infielders at all positions, with a right-handed coach or pitcher on the mound.
3. Signal to runners whether you want them to steal second and hold at third or delay-steal at first and send the runner on third home.
4. The pitcher or coach gets set, checks the runner, and throws home.
5. The offense runs a play and reacts to the defense.
6. Rotate the groups after five to ten minutes.

▌ Key Points

- When the runner at third is holding, he should shorten his lead and not fake to home until after the ball passes the pitcher's mound.
- If there are two outs, the runner at first must not get tagged out on a delay steal until the runner on third scores.
- When the runner at third is going to break, he must go as the catcher releases the ball.
- The runner on third must be alert for throws back to the pitcher, upon which he must stop and get back to third.

First-and-Third Steal Drill: RHP

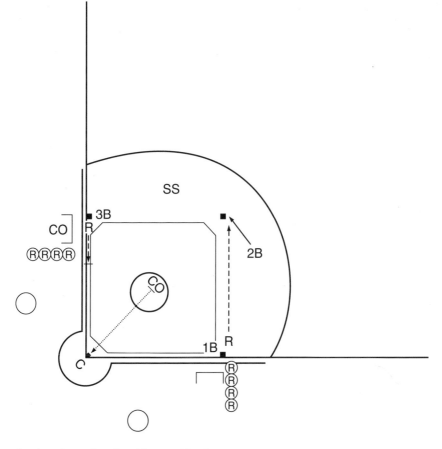

Stealing Second and Holding at Third

Straight-Line Drill

▌ Purpose

To execute the crossover step and head in a straight line to the next base

▌ Equipment

Grassy area and outfield foul lines or a white chalk line drawn in the outfield grass

▌ Procedure

1. Runners line up with the left foot perpendicular to the foul line and the right foot (from toe to instep) at a 45° angle from the line.

2. On the coach's command, cross over with your left foot landing on the chalk line. Keep running down the line.

3. Each stride should land on the chalk line.

▌ Key Points

- As you line up, you can drop your right foot back a little, just behind the line.

- Start slow and pick up the pace.

- When you cross over with your left foot, you should be directly on the chalk line.

Straight-Line Drill

Returning to Base

▌ Purpose

To learn how to dive back to first, second, or third base

▌ Equipment

Foul line in outfield and grassy area with throw-down bases

▌ Procedure

1. Line up about 10 feet away from the line, taking a lead off first base.

2. A coach or player stands about 20 feet in front of you and comes to the set position (not shown in photo).

3. When the coach or player gets set and fakes a throw back to first, dive back to the bag, using proper form.

▌ Key Points

- Take your lead on the outfield side of the base.
- Take one step and dive back to the base.
- When you dive back to the base, touch the back corner of the base with your right hand.
- To avoid jarring your shoulder, hit your hand on the ground three to four inches in front of the base and slide into the base.

▌ Variation

As an alternative to the dive, come back to first standing up, using the proper form.

Returning to Base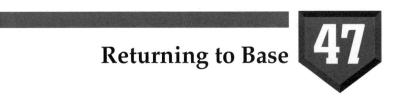

Sliding Drill

▌ Purpose

To develop proper sliding technique and eliminate fear of sliding

▌ Equipment

Throw-down bases and grassy area

▌ Procedure

1. Wet down the area without getting too much standing water.
2. Pair up players.
3. One player sits on his side and buttocks, extending his lead leg and tucking his other leg under; his partner pulls him several feet. Players take turns pulling and sliding.

▌ Key Points

- This drill is especially valuable on rainy days.
- It's easier to slide on the buttocks than on the side.
- Wet the field but be careful that the players still have some control while sliding.

▌ Variations

Players can try variations of the bent-leg slide.

Players can also try the head-first slide.

Sliding Drill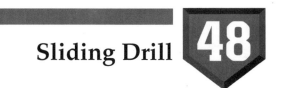

Bent-Leg Slide

Stealing Home

▌ Purpose

To learn the proper techniques of stealing home

▌ Equipment

Infield area or outfield or gym (using throw-down bases)

▌ Procedure

1. The runner takes a stealing lead from third while focusing on the pitcher.
2. The pitcher winds up and throws to the catcher.
3. A hitter at home shows bunt.
4. Go through this setup several times, then let the runner attempt to steal home.

▌ Key Points

- Use four runners at a time to speed up the drill and involve more players.
- The pitcher should use several different deliveries to the plate: no look, look, and then slow to plate.
- Make the drill simulate game conditions. Use a pitcher, catcher, batter, and runner. Runners should slide as in a game.
- Successful attempts will give players cofidence to steal home in a game.

Stealing Home

49

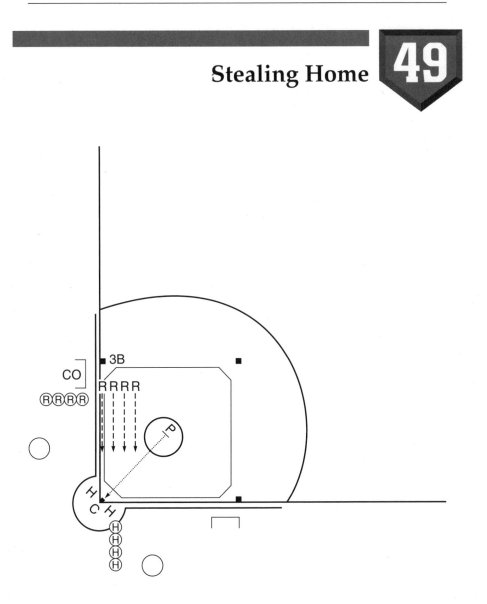

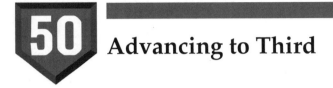

Advancing to Third

▌ Purpose

To learn when and how to advance to third base

▌ Equipment

Baseball and fungo bat

▌ Procedure

1. A complete infield is in place for defense.

2. Two runners at a time are on second base. Runners line up at the base.

3. Using a fungo bat, a coach hits the ball between third and short, directly at the runners or to their left.

4. The runners read the ball, checking whether it is in front of or behind them to determine whether they can advance to third.

▌ Key Points

- Hit some line drives that the third baseman and shortstop can catch.
- Hit some slow rollers to help the runners react to these as well.

Advancing to Third 50

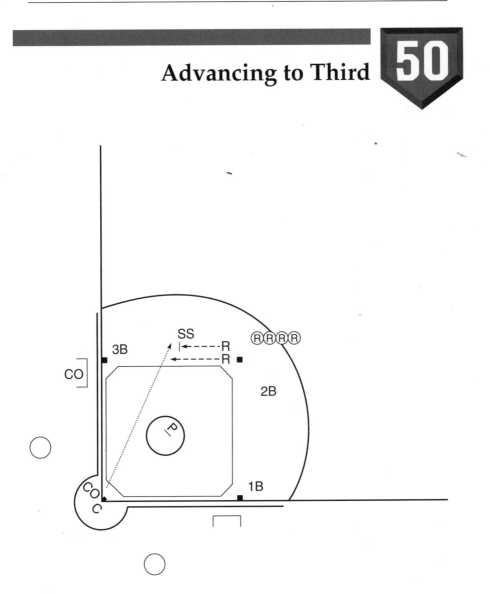

Stealing Third

▮ Purpose

To learn how to steal third base

▮ Equipment

Balls, pitcher, catcher, middle infielders

▮ Procedure

1. A pitcher is on the mound and three runners are at second base.

2. The pitcher comes to a set position and goes through his routine (one look or two looks, etc.).

3. The runners read the pitcher, slide up the baseline with a secondary lead, and steal third.

▮ Key Points

- Runners should shuffle off toward third, adding to the primary lead before breaking for third.

- Change the pitching rhythm or the pitcher's looks at the runners so the runners can practice different scenarios.

- Try picks at second base with the middle infielders.

- Add a coach at third to help the runners with the middle infielders.

Stealing Third 51

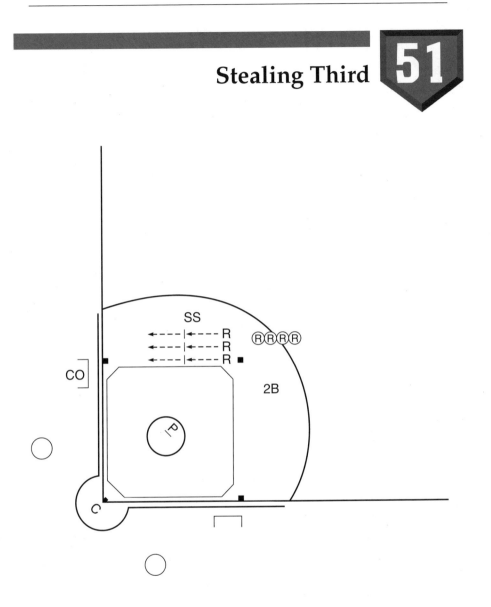

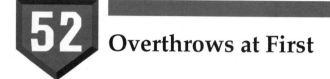

52 Overthrows at First

▌ Purpose

To learn how to react to an overthrow at first base

▌ Equipment

Infield or grassy area and base

▌ Procedure

1. Players line up at home.
2. A coach is in fair territory on the infield grass, about eight to ten feet away from first base.
3. A first baseman is in position.
4. The first player at home runs down the first base line.
5. The player runs through the base and glances over his right shoulder on his first step past the base.
6. The coach throws a ball over the first baseman's head.
7. The runner sees the wild throw and advances to second if possible.

▌ Key Points

- Alternate good and wild throws to keep the players from automatically breaking toward second base.
- Runners should run through first base full speed, just as in a game.
- After running through first base, the runner should slow and spread his stride to allow a quicker break toward second if it's possible to advance.

Overthrows at First

52

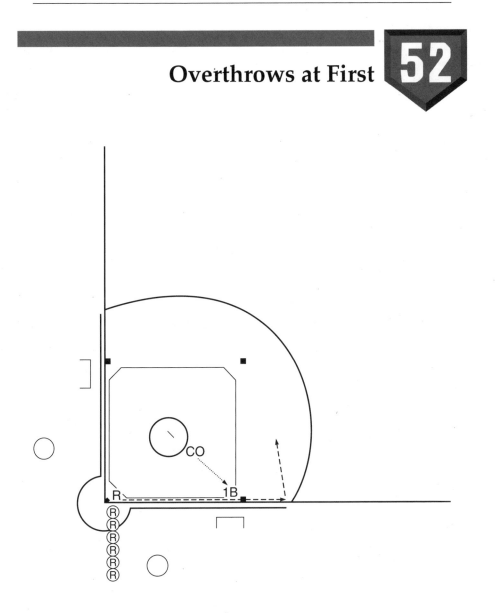

Baserunning Conditioning Drill

▌ Purpose

To condition your players by having them run the bases in game-like situations

▌ Equipment

Bases and infield or indoor facility

▌ Procedure

1. Sprint from home through first base, as if you've just hit a ground ball in the infield.

2. Take a lead at first and execute a delay steal of second.

3. Take a one-out lead from second and score on a base hit.

4. From home plate, make a turn at first base, simulating a base hit to the outfield.

5. Simulate a hit-and-run, taking your normal lead at first base and ending up at third.

6. Tag up on a fly ball to left field and sprint home.

7. Execute back-to-back doubles and two scores from second base.

8. End with an inside-the-park home run.

▌ Key Points

- Keep the players moving. This drill should not last more than five and a half minutes.

- Add a few more plays as you desire, such as stealing second or third.

- After you tell players, "Inside-the-park home run, last one," inform them that they tied the game—and they have to run one more. This helps develop mental toughness.

Baserunning Conditioning Drill **53**

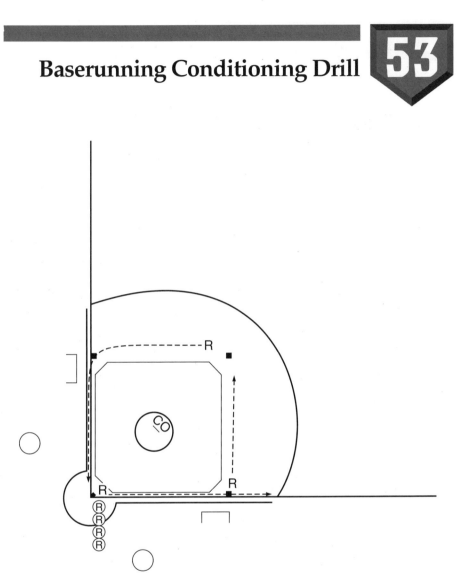

Procedures #1, 2, and 3

Dirt-Ball Reads

▮ Purpose

To learn how to read the ball in the dirt and react to the play

▮ Equipment

Baseballs, infield or gym, helmets

▮ Procedure

1. Divide your players equally at first, second, and third base.
2. Runners take primary leads and then secondary leads as you throw to the catcher.
3. The runners read the ball to see if it will be in the dirt.
4. The runners advance if they can.

▮ Key Points

- This is a great indoor drill to use during inclement weather.
- Runners should track the ball from the mound to the plate.
- The runner on first should be more aggressive than the runners at second and third because the throw to second is the longest for the catcher.
- Place infielders at second and third for the catcher to throw to. Runners should wear helmets for their protection.

Dirt-Ball Reads

54

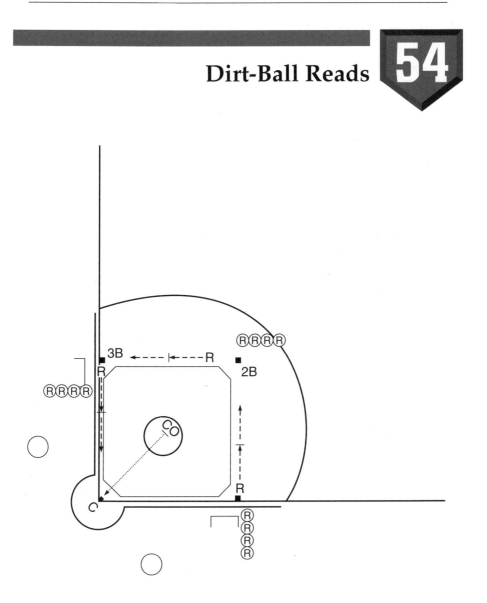

Reads at Second

▌ Purpose

To learn how to tag up at second

▌ Equipment

Fungo bat, balls, baseball field

▌ Procedure

1. Place several runners at second base and run them two at a time.
2. A coach is at home plate with a fungo bat.
3. Outfielders are in position.
4. The coach hits fungoes, line drives, and pop-ups to the outfield and the runners react accordingly, either holding or advancing to the next base.

▌ Key Points

- Conduct the drill at full speed.
- Occasionally have the outfielders bobble some balls to see if the runners are really paying attention.
- Runners should try to learn their limitations and strengths in advancing to the next base.

▌ Variation

Add a third base coach to give him practice also.

Reads at Second

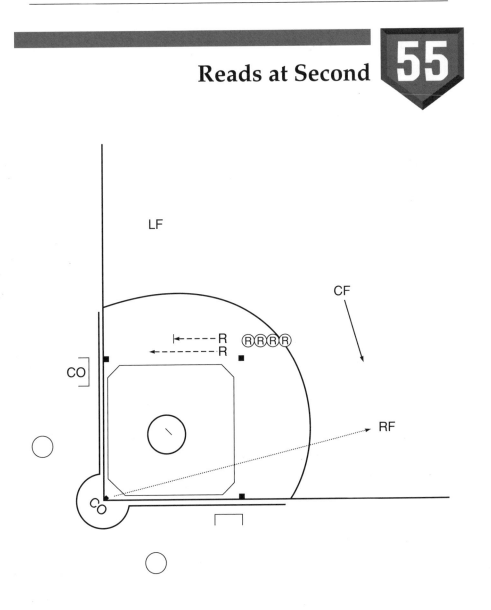

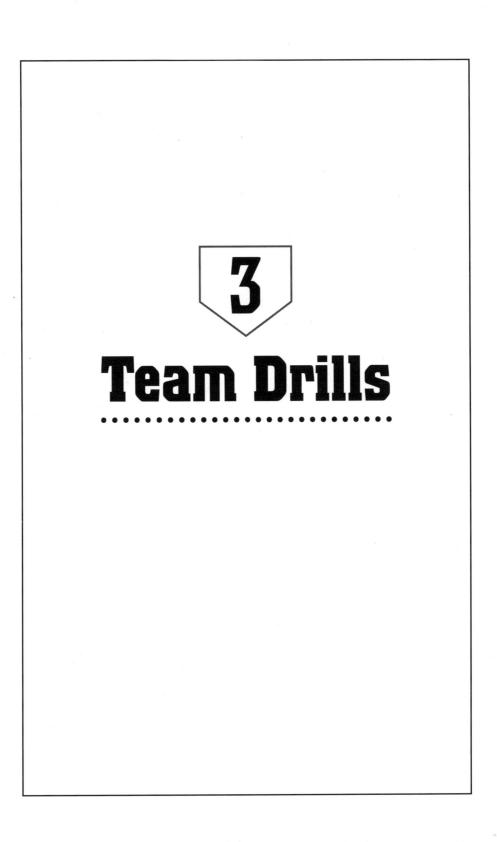

3

Team Drills

3

Team Drills

• • • • • • • • • • • • • • • • • • • •

Although individual hitting and baserunning skills are essential, baseball is at its best when players combine their respective skills into a coordinated offensive attack. Baseball is, after all, a team sport. And the team aspect involves not only learning and executing skills, but executing them at the right time.

The suicide squeeze is a perfect example of this critical timing factor. The runner on third breaks for the plate, trusting in his teammate at home to put the ball in play on the ground. If one of the two players fails his assignment, the play has little chance of success. But, when executed correctly, the play is almost impossible to stop.

The hit-and-run, bunt-and-run, and slash bunt are three more plays that involve the proper execution and precise timing of skills by two or more players. In chapters 1 and 2, we practiced the offensive techniques required in such plays. In this chapter, the focus shifts to synchronizing the performance of those skills with teammates in game situations.

The 13 drills that follow will develop the precise timing and skills players need to execute important baseball strategies, such as learning how to tag up in a first-and-third situation, how to hit to the opposite field with a runner on first, how to react to the ball as a runner on third base, and many more. If you want to take full advantage of run-scoring opportunities, work on these tactics regularly in practice.

ATEC Intrasquad Drill

▍ Purpose

To simulate game-like hitting conditions, giving players practice hitting curveballs and fastballs

▍ Equipment

L-shaped screen, ATEC pitching machine, balls, bats, helmets

▍ Procedure

1. Place a fielder at each defensive position and four players on offense.
2. Feed the ATEC pitching machine while standing behind the protective screen. Raise both arms and show the hitter the ball before dropping only one ball into the machine. This way the hitter can't guess which pitch is coming.
3. The player at bat runs after hitting the ball.
4. Both offensive and defensive players react to plays just as in a game.

▍ Key Points

- Mix in both curveballs and fastballs to simulate game-like conditions.
- Rotate players between defense and offense so all get a chance to hit.
- Use base coaches and have the third base coach flash signs.
- Don't allow stealing, but execute other plays such as the hit-and-run, squeeze, and so on.

ATEC Intrasquad Drill

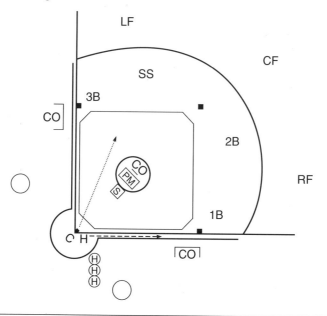

ATEC Pitching Machine

57 Tri-Station Drill

▌ Purpose

To maximize the number of reps on offense for each player

▌ Equipment

Field, batting cage, L-shaped screens, bats, balls, ATEC pitching machine

▌ Procedure

1. Set up three stations: live hitting, bunting down the right field line, and cage work.

2. Limit the groups to four or five players in every station, allowing each hitter four or five minutes.

3. Players work in one station for 20 minutes and then jog over to the next station to avoid wasting time.

▌ Key Points

- In the bunting station, put down cones and chart players' success ratio.

- Although players will be shifting from station to station, emphasize correct technique and concentration in each of the three hitting stations.

▌ Variations

Add a fourth station: defense. Adjust the time for each station to 15 minutes or keep it at 20.

Another station you could add is a hit-by-pitch station.

Tri-Station Drill 57

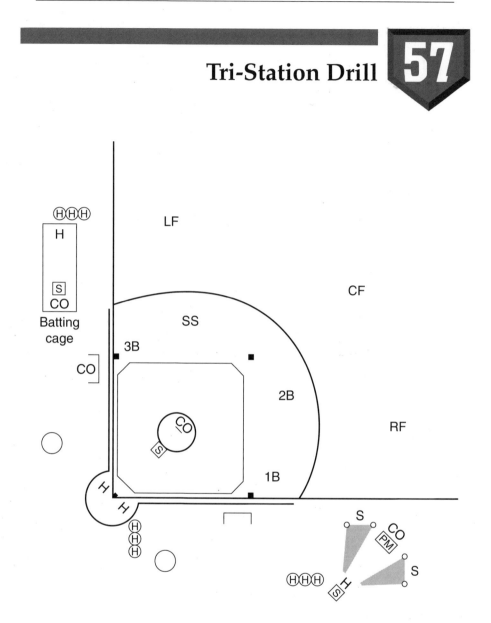

58 Bunt-and-Run Drill

▌ Purpose

To practice both defensive and offensive skills on bunts down the first and third base lines

▌ Equipment

Field, baseballs, bats, helmets

▌ Procedure

1. Place players in all nine defensive positions.
2. Place a runner on each base and have a batter bunt the ball.
3. Position a coach on the first base line for right-handed bunters and third base line for left-handed bunters, both about 15 feet from the hitter.
4. The pitcher winds up without a ball and simulates a throw while one of the coaches tosses the ball for the hitter to bunt.
5. The runners react to the bunted ball and try to advance to the next base.

▌ Key Points

- This is a great drill when the pitchers' arms are too tender to throw hard.
- Outfielders should back up bases.
- Throw hard enough so the ball will come off the bat as it would in a game.
- Occasionally have the hitter miss a bunt to make sure the runners don't cross over toward the next base until they see the ball on the ground.

Bunt-and-Run Drill 58

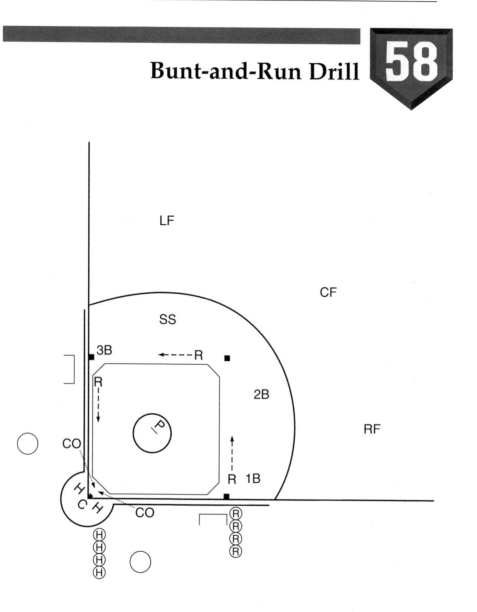

Opposite-Field Scrimmage

▍ Purpose

To hit the outside pitch with a consistent, grooved swing, driving the ball to the opposite field

▍ Equipment

ATEC pitching machine, bats, balls, helmets, screen

▍ Procedure

1. A defensive team is in place and four offensive players will hit and run the bases.

2. Set up an ATEC pitching machine to throw balls on the outside of the plate, mixing in both fastballs and curveballs.

3. The hitter hits to the opposite field, and the defense reacts to the hit.

4. Players get three at-bats and then rotate to a defensive position.

▍ Key Points

- Players should try to hit line drives or hard ground balls. Mix in a push or drag bunt to the right side of the diamond to move a runner or to get a base hit.

- Set up different offensive situations by putting runners on the bases.

- If a batter pops up, have him sprint to the right field wall while the next hitter is up.

Opposite-Field Scrimmage 59

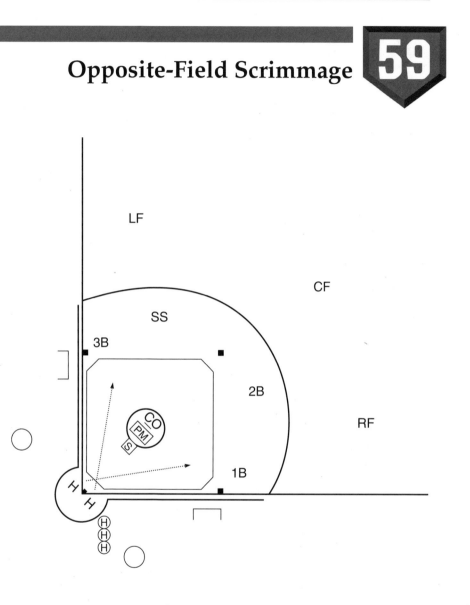

Squeeze Drill

▌ Purpose

To practice game-action bunting techniques

▌ Equipment

Bats, balls, infield area

▌ Procedure

1. A batter is at the plate with a pitcher, catcher, and infield in place and two runners at third base. The runners go two at a time with one runner in foul territory.

2. A third base coach is in the box to make sure the runners don't leave early.

3. The runners break for home after the pitcher breaks his hands and his motion toward the plate begins.

4. The hitter bunts the ball in fair territory and the defense reacts to the ball, either throwing home or to first base.

▌ Key Points

- Runners shouldn't break toward the plate too early; this will alert the defense to the play.

- Runners or hitters who don't execute properly should sprint down the right field line. Knowing this is the consequence may help them focus on executing properly.

- The bunter should bunt the ball where it is pitched. A right-hander should bunt an outside pitch toward first and an inside pitch toward third.

- Use this drill for both suicide and safety squeeze bunts.

Squeeze Drill 60

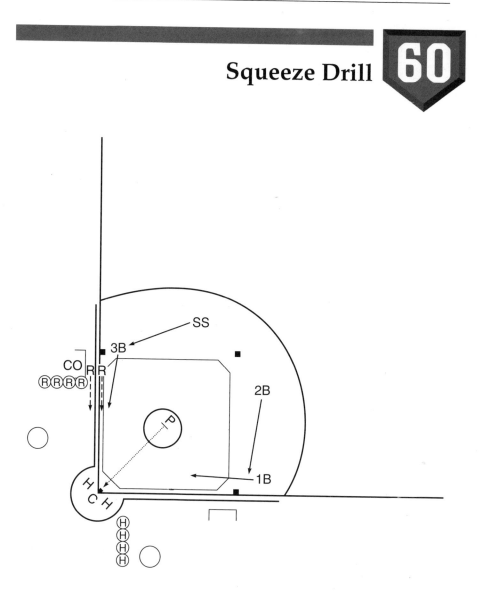

61 Tag-Up Drill: First and Third

▮ Purpose

To learn how to tag up at first and third and advance in a game situation

▮ Equipment

Baseball field, fungo, baseballs

▮ Procedure

1. Runners are on first and third.
2. Fielders are in position in the outfield and infield.
3. A coach at home plate hits fly balls to the outfield.
4. Runners take leads and react to the ball hit by the coach.
5. Runners read the catch and then break for the next base as the outfielder makes the proper throw.
6. The pitcher backs up home plate.

▮ Key Points

- Hit different types of fly balls in this drill: short, medium, and long.
- The two other outfielders should tell the outfielder catching the ball where to throw.
- Middle infielders should yell, "Two, two, two," telling the outfielder to throw to second base, on balls hit deep with no play at the plate.

Tag-Up Drill: First and Third

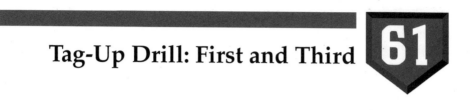

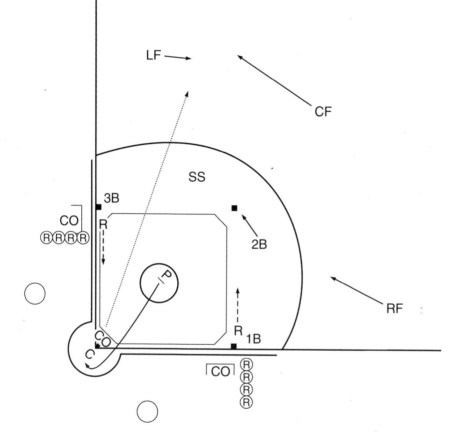

Slash Bunt Drill

▌ Purpose

To develop the skill to slash bunt

▌ Equipment

Bats, balls, batting tunnel or infield area, screens

Procedure

1. A complete infield is in place.

2. Pitcher throws from the mound (or a pitching coach throws from 45 feet away), behind an L-shaped screen for protection.

3. Runners are at first and second.

4. A screen between third and home, about 15 feet away from the plate, protects the third baseman, who will break with the pitch toward home.

5. The hitter shows bunt, the pitcher checks the runners and throws to the plate, and the defense charges in.

6. The hitter pulls the bat straight back, and with a choked-up grip and short stroke, drives the ball through the shortstop hole.

Key Points

- Emphasize pitch selection. Hitters should swing at strikes only.

- Occasionally switch the defensive strategy. When the defense doesn't charge in, the hitter should respond by bunting the ball.

- Hitters should try to hit a slow ground ball through the shortstop hole. This gives the runner at first a chance to reach third base.

- To add some incentive, have the hitter sprint to the right field wall and back if he doesn't execute.

Slash Bunt Drill

62

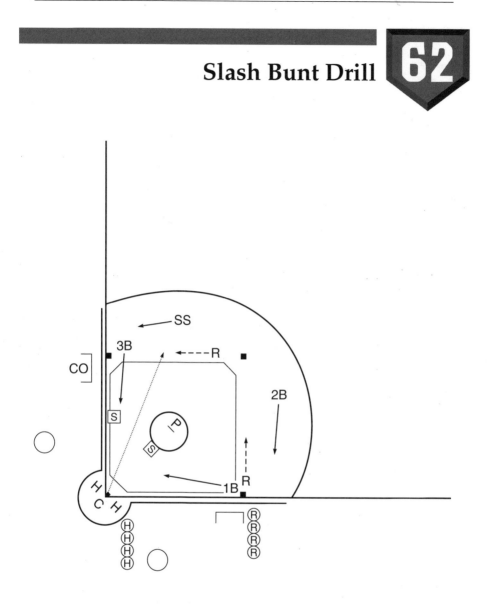

Runner on Second

▌ Purpose

To learn how to advance a runner to third base

▌ Equipment

Baseball field, screen, bat, balls, helmets (pitching machine is optional)

▌ Procedure

1. First, second, and third basemen are in place and a runner is on second.

2. The outfielders are behind the cage at home, with one hitter hitting while the others wait in line. Hitters and runners should wear helmets.

3. A coach is on the mound behind an L-shaped screen, either throwing or feeding the pitching machine.

4. The hitter hits the ball to the right side of the diamond to move the runner to third base.

5. Mix in a few drag or push bunts to advance the runner.

▌ Key Points

- Hitters should work on hitting either ground balls to the right side or deep fly balls to advance the runner.
- A bunt increases the odds of advancing the runner to third.
- Right-handed hitters should look for an outside pitch they can drive the other way.
- Left-handed hitters should look for an inside pitch they can pull.
- Hitters who don't execute should sprint.

Runner on Second 63

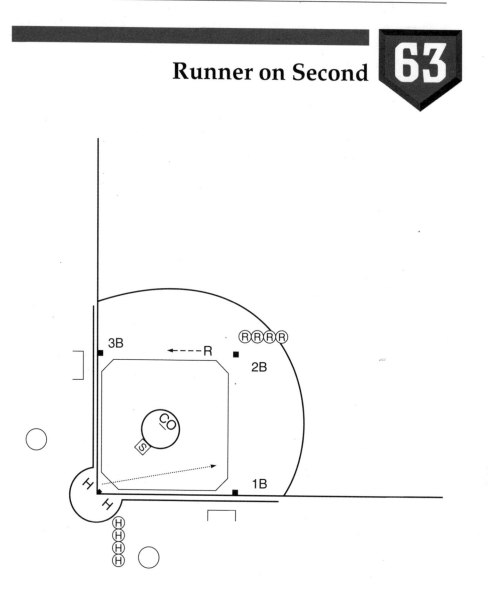

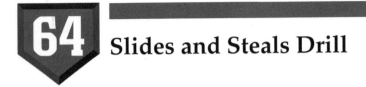

Slides and Steals Drill

▌ Purpose

To review various slides and steals, including bent leg, pop up, head first, back door, and pop tag

▌ Equipment

Infield and bases

▌ Procedure

1. Divide players into four groups: one group each at home, first, second, and third.

2. The group at home works on reading the first baseman coming off the bag and avoiding a tag by using the pop-tag slide method.

3. The group at first works on stealing second, using either a bent-leg slide or a pop-tag slide.

4. The group at second works on stealing third, using the head-first slide.

5. The group at third works on stealing home, using the pop-up slide. Also have this group work on pop-tag and back-door slides as if they were scoring from second.

6. Rotate stations every three minutes, and rotate groups of runners after about 15 minutes.

▌ Key Points

- Coaches should cover each station.
- Put dirt around the bases to give the runners a little added protection.

▌ Variation

The second baseman or shortstop simulates an overthrow to first and the runner uses a pop-up slide.

Slides and Steals Drill 64

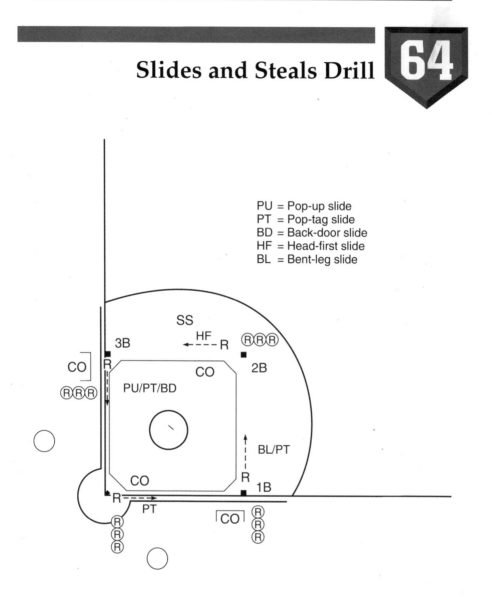

PU = Pop-up slide
PT = Pop-tag slide
BD = Back-door slide
HF = Head-first slide
BL = Bent-leg slide

Runner on Third

▌ Purpose

To learn how to react to balls off the bat in a game situation

▌ Equipment

Helmets, baseballs, bats, baseball field

▌ Procedure

1. A full defense is in position.
2. Two runners are at third and two hitters are in the cage.
3. The hitter tries to get the runner in from third with less than two outs by bunting or hitting away.
4. The runners at third should go one at a time, each reacting to the ball off the bat.

▌ Key Points

- The runner should freeze and tag up on all balls in the air.
- Use a third base coach to instruct the runner to go or stay on ground balls.
- Instruct runners to take a lead in foul territory—if the ball hits the runner in foul territory, he's not out.

Runner on Third   65

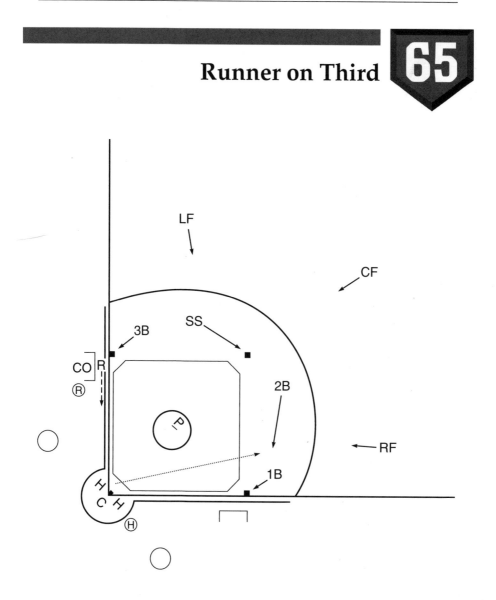

Two-Strike Drill

▌ Purpose

To learn to protect the plate when there are two strikes

▌ Equipment

Helmets, L-shaped screen, mat, baseballs, field, pitching machine (optional)

▌ Procedure

1. Set up the L-shaped screen 40 to 45 feet away from home plate. Put down a mat under the screen to avoid damaging the grass.

2. Set up a defense and have one hitter in the cage with two hitters on deck.

3. The hitter looks outside and tries to adjust to the pitcher's inside throw, make contact, and put the ball in play.

4. Rotate the fielders from defense to offense to allow everyone to hit.

▌ Key Points

- Hitters should focus on the ball away, but be ready to react on an inside pitch.

- If a hitter swings and misses or swings at a ball out of the strike zone, the next hitter steps in.

- Occasionally run the count to 3 and 2. This focuses the duel between the pitcher and the hitter.

Two-Strike Drill **66**

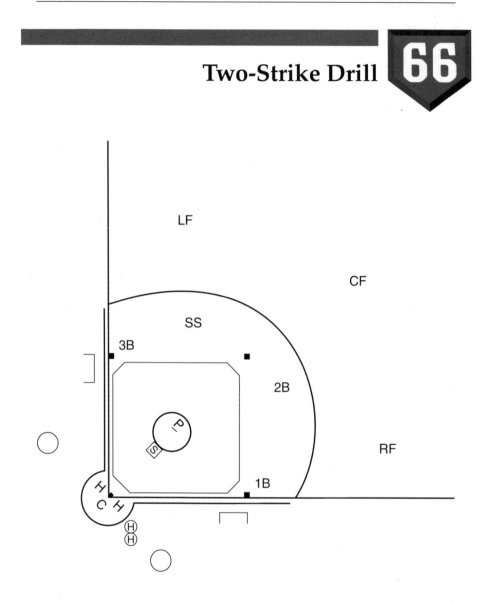

Hit-and-Run Drill

▌ Purpose

To learn how to execute the hit-and-run both as a baserunner and as a hitter

▌ Equipment

Baseball field, bat, balls, L-shaped screen, cage

▌ Procedure

1. Divide your team into two groups: outfielders at first base, infielders at home. A coach stands on the mound behind an L-shaped screen.

2. Using the cage for a backstop, the coach gets set and throws to the hitter.

3. The runner on first breaks when the coach delivers the pitch.

4. The runner on first should glance toward the plate as he breaks for second, looking for a pitchout. He should again glance on his third or fourth step to see if the ball was hit on the ground or in the air.

5. The hitter tries to stay on top of the ball and hit a line drive or a hard grounder.

6. Rotate infielders and outfielders after three to five minutes.

▌ Key Points

- The hitter should hit the ball anywhere except to the middle.
- Players who fail to execute at either spot should sprint to the right field wall and back.

Hit-and-Run Drill

67

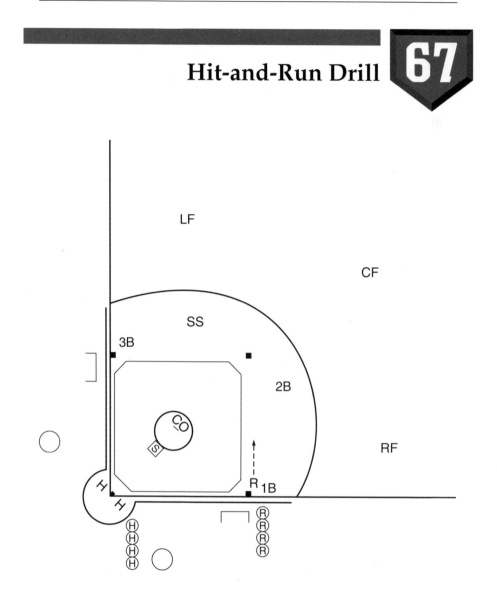

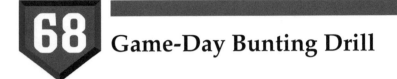

68   Game-Day Bunting Drill

▌ Purpose

To practice the base-hit bunting technique in a game situation

▌ Equipment

Infield, baseballs, bats, cones

▌ Procedure

1. Mark lines down the first and third base lines that indicate where to bunt the ball. Cones can also be used to mark off a certain area.

2. A pitcher, catcher, and infield are in place. Outfielders are optional.

3. Each hitter works on the techniques of bunting for a base hit, trying to bunt the ball in the designated areas.

4. A player gets one chance to bunt the ball into the designated areas. Then rotate.

▌ Key Points

• Infielders shouldn't move until the hitter shows bunt.

• Hitters shouldn't run out of the box before they bunt.

• Location of the bunt is more important than getting a great jump out of the box.

Game-Day Bunting Drill

68

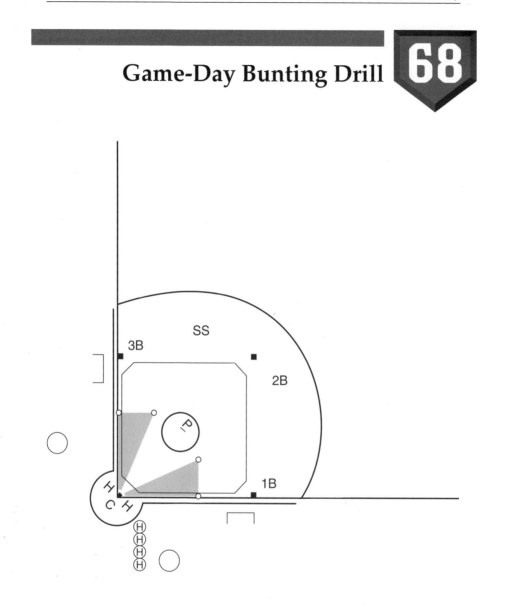

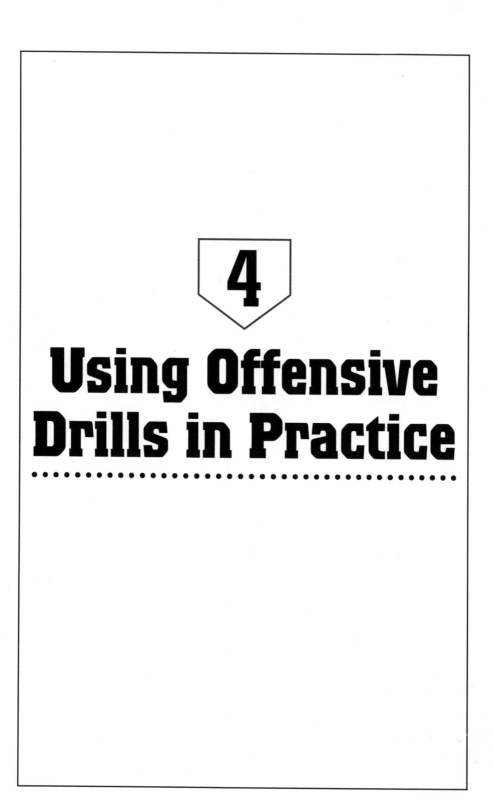

4

Using Offensive Drills in Practice

4
Using Offensive Drills in Practice

●●●●●●●●●●●●●●●●●●●●●●●●●●●●●●●●●

Think of some of the great offensive players in baseball today. Guys like Ken Griffey, Jr., Frank Thomas, and Barry Bonds probably come to mind. These are athletes who seem to perform difficult skills effortlessly and smoothly, as if it just comes naturally to them.

In reality, even the greatest players practice many hours to develop and polish the skills they display in games. And most players, probably 99 percent, have to work even harder than that to be successful.

One of the best hitters today, Tony Gwynn, is a great example of this. Gwynn has won batting titles not because of his natural athletic ability but because of his strong work ethic and careful study of opposing pitchers. Similarly, the great Lou Brock was so dedicated in his conditioning and learned pitchers' deliveries so well that he made base stealing look easy.

Every baseball player who has achieved high-level, long-term success did so by practicing hard and smart. The motivation to work at the game must come from within the player. The "smarts" involves applying the drills presented in the first three chapters in your practice sessions. In this chapter, we'll show you how to use the drills to the greatest benefit.

Using Drills Effectively

We've all had bad baseball practices—days where nothing seems to go right. If you coach or play the game long enough, it's bound to happen. What is far less understandable is why any player or coach would guarantee a poor practice experience. Why would anyone, for example, set up a drill where all of the players stand in a single-file line, waiting for their turn to participate? And what's the point in performing drills that involve no use of the skills needed to be successful in a game, or that are so difficult or easy that their only real effect is to demotivate players?

This is an area in which baseball coaching could improve. After learning how to execute the drill, players need repetitive practice of the right skills, using the right drills, at the right level of difficulty. The 68 drills presented in this book must be used wisely in order to enhance a player's performance. Here are the keys to using drills effectively.

Make the Conditions of the Drill as Game-Like as Possible

This will focus your players on the situation at hand, make the drill more interesting, and prepare them for facing the same situation in a game. Players tend to coast on drills that aren't game-like, because they don't see how the drills apply to actual competition.

Even when you're having your players run, rather than having them run the foul lines, have them sprint the bases. This gives more meaning to the conditioning, adds life to the drill, and gives them a feel for what they'll be doing in games.

Determine Whether the Drill Is at the Appropriate Skill Level

Most of the drills in this book can, with sometimes minor modification, be performed by players at all levels. But some are easier than others. What drills you'll begin with and what drills you'll progress to will depend on the experience and skill levels of players and their development as the season moves on.

Structure the Drills to Maximize Player Repetitions Over a Short Time

This will not only help players learn and hone the skills they're practicing, but also make the drill more active and interesting. Mental preparation is so important in baseball, and drills that are properly paced, with many players active, help players develop mental alertness and aggressiveness. If players become bored, you've waited too long to step in and change things.

Increase the Demands of the Drills

Another way to help players develop both physically and mentally is to increase the demands of the drill once they have learned how to execute its fundamentals. For instance, you could require your players to perform the drill faster, or with fewer errors, or introduce an opponent.

An example of how to do this is "Getting a Jump" (Drill #37). At first, players practice getting a good jump off first base as the pitcher throws home. Later, have the runner on first attempt to steal, with middle infielders in place. Many drills can be adapted to increase the demands on the players. And doing so will keep them mentally sharp, add variety and intensity to the practice, and allow them to experience more game-like situations.

Develop Drill Performance Criteria to Gauge Players' Improvement

Finally, come up with some way to evaluate performance in drills to see where improvement has occurred and where it still needs to take place. Developing performance criteria helps you determine

- when it's time to move on to another drill or to increase the demand of the drill,
- players' present skill level,
- which skills players need extra help with, and
- which drills to use for players' continued improvement.

Most of the drills, especially the hitting drills, can be used in informal practice settings as well as formal team practices. Two players can perform many of the drills together, making them practical for off-season workouts as well as in-season practices.

Sample Practice Plans

During the season, coaches should plan their team workouts. The practice plans should take into account all of the factors we've considered—players' skill levels, special areas of improvement, game-like situations, and so on. Scheduling is another concern. To see how these factors can be adjusted to fit the situation, let's compare sample practice plans for youth, intermediate, and advanced baseball teams.

Youth Baseball Programs

Until high school, most kids aren't very serious about the game. They love to play it, but the concentration isn't there. Nor is the development of some basic skills needed to perform the more difficult drills.

Transportation is another issue. Unless the entire team lives close to the ballpark, the kids will need an adult to deliver them to the practice site.

A final consideration is time. When do you schedule practices so that everyone can attend, and how long do the practice sessions last? In many cases, the league will set both the number of practices and the length of the practices (because of facility availability). It's common for youth baseball teams to have only an hour per practice.

The sample practice plans on pages 160 and 161 take all of these factors into account. Use them as is or modify the plans to best meet your team's needs.

SAMPLE PRACTICE PLAN—YOUTH TEAM

MONDAY / WEDNESDAY / FRIDAY	
5:30 p.m.	Warm up, stretch, and throw
5:40 p.m.	**Tri-Station Drill — #57** (three groups, 10 minutes each station)
6:10 p.m.	Defensive infield and outfield work (two groups, rotate after 10 minutes)
6:30 p.m.	Team meeting, end practice

TUESDAY / THURSDAY	
5:00 p.m.	Warm up, stretch, and throw
5:10 p.m.	Live hitting and **Hit-Stick Drill — #26** (two groups, rotate after 10 minutes)
5:30 p.m.	Defensive infield and outfield work (two groups, rotate after 10 minutes)
5:50 p.m.	**Reaction Drill — #38** **Advancing to Second — #39**
5:55 p.m.	**Three Stops Drill — #44**
6:00 p.m.	Team meeting, end practice

Intermediate and Advanced Baseball Programs

High school, legion, college, semi-pro, and certainly professional players all take the game seriously. It's more than a pasttime for them. Because of this greater commitment and the fact that the players are old enough to drive, scheduling practices shouldn't be a problem. Nor does practice time have to be so limited, as players at this level are much more developed physically and can withstand longer and harder workouts.

Intermediate and advanced teams often have more than one coach. Multiple coaches, used effectively, can make practices much more efficient. Smaller, multiple stations can be used for drills so that each player gets more reps in less minutes. The Team Drills practice segment included in the advanced team practice plan (see pp. 163-164) is an example of this. It is great for game preparation because you're working on executing game strategies in game-like situations, but it also allows for individual attention to skill development and correction.

At this level of baseball, players' skills may be highly advanced in some areas, but weak in others. Tailoring a practice that meets the needs of all the athletes on the team can be difficult when such a wide range of skills are involved. The challenge is to allow enough flexibility to test the highly talented players performing the skill they do best and still not overwhelm less talented players working on deficient skills.

With all of these concerns in mind, along with the five key points presented earlier in this chapter, let's look at how you might structure practices for intermediate and advanced players.

SAMPLE PRACTICE PLAN—INTERMEDIATE TEAM

5:00 p.m.	Warm up and stretch
5:10 p.m.	Throw
5:20 p.m.	Cutoffs and relays • double cuts • runners on first and second
5:40 p.m.	Quad stations (15 minutes each, groups rotating) • live hitting—opposite field • cage work—Decker baseballs • bunting—right field line **(Bunting Technique — #8)** • defense—ground balls
6:40 p.m.	**Three Stops Drill — #44**
6:55 p.m.	Team meeting—mental aspects
7:00 p.m.	End practice

SAMPLE PRACTICE PLAN—ADVANCED TEAM

2:00 p.m.	Warm up and stretch
2:07 p.m.	Throw
2:15 p.m.	Quick hands
2:20 p.m.	Bunting stations • push • drag • safety (**Bunting Technique — #8**) • sacrifice (**Bunting Technique — #8**)
2:30 p.m.	Cutoffs and relays (pitchers run) • double cuts • runners on first and second • runners on first and third—fly balls
2:50 p.m.	Team Drills (**pick any two team drills: #56, #57, #59, #61**, or **#64**)
3:25 p.m.	Break
3:30 p.m.	Quad station (**Tri-Station Drill — #57**) (15 minutes each) • live hitting • bunting • cage work • defense
4:30 p.m.	**Hit-and-Run Drill — #67**
4:50 p.m.	Reads • at first base—stealing second (**Reading Pitcher's Moves — #36**)

(continued)

(continued)

	• at second base—stealing third **(Stealing Third — #51)**
	• at third base—stealing home **(Stealing Home — #49)**
	• on dirt balls **(Dirt-Ball Reads — #54)**
5:35 p.m.	**Three Stops Drill — #44**
5:55 p.m.	Team meeting—mental aspects
6:00 p.m.	End practice

The Bottom Line

Amidst all the details about drills and practice plans, let's not lose sight of their purpose. Both are meant to improve player performance. The goal isn't to run every drill and every practice perfectly. It's to use drills as effectively as possible during practice to develop players' skills.

What really matters is what happens when players step between the lines on game day. That's the bottom line of this book. The drills should prepare players to excel in every offensive area and in every possible game situation. And that means more runs, more rallies, and more wins!

About the Author

Rod Delmonico became head baseball coach at the University of Tennessee in 1989. In his first six seasons he led the Vols to three consecutive Southeastern Conference (SEC) Eastern Division titles, two consecutive SEC overall titles, and a 1995 trip to the College World Series (the school's first in 44 years). His many coaching honors include SEC Coach of the Year (1994 and 1995), American Baseball Coaches Association's South Region Coach of the Year (1995), and *Baseball America*'s Coach of the Year (1995).

Rod also was associated with two of the nation's top collegiate programs, spending six seasons as assistant coach at Florida State University and two seasons as a graduate assistant at Clemson University.

Rod earned a master's degree in administration and supervision from Clemson University (1983).

A popular figure at coaching clinics throughout the nation, Rod was recently the featured speaker at the American Baseball Coaches Association Clinic. He is a contributing author to numerous coaching periodicals. His articles have been published in *Scholastic Coach* and *Collegiate Baseball* magazines and his first instructional book, *Hit and Run Baseball*, is now in its second printing.

6 More Resources to Improve Your Season

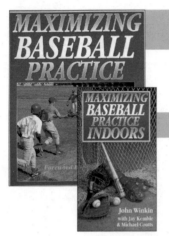

John Winkin with Jay Kemble and Michael Coutts

Foreword by Tommy Lasorda

1995 • Paper • 152 pp • Item PWIN0430
ISBN 0-87322-430-2 • $17.95 ($23.95 Canadian)

(88-minute videotape)

1995 • 1/2" VHS • Item MWIN0438
ISBN 0-88011-485-1 • $29.95 ($44.95 Canadian)

Special Book and Video Package
1/2" VHS and *Maximizing Baseball Practice* book
Item MWIN0446 • ISBN 0-88011-496-7
$44.95 ($67.50 Canadian)

This book shows how to make the most of a squad's allotted practice time and space. It contains dozens of illustrated drills designed to give players the gamelike experiences and repetitions they need to compete successfully. It also provides a menu of options and strategies that can be easily adapted to different coaching philosophies.

The companion videotape demonstrates how to conduct effective indoor practices. It's loaded with drills and drill variations for improving defensive and offensive skills.

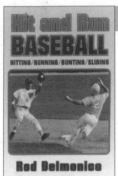

Rod Delmonico, MEd

Foreword by Ron Fraser

1992 • Paper • 184 pp • Item PDEL0327
ISBN 0-88011-327-8 • $15.95 ($22.50 Canadian)

Provides the basic skills and the advanced insights needed to develop an aggressive baseball offense. Contains over 200 sequenced pictures showing positioning, footwork, and technique. And every chapter concludes with mental tips for players and skill-specific drills—25 in all!

Watch for us on-line March 1, 1996!
http://www.hkusa.com

Human Kinetics
The Premier Publisher for Sports & Fitness

2335

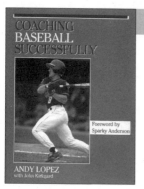

Andy Lopez with John Kirkgard

Foreword by George "Sparky" Anderson

1996 • Paper • Approx 208 pp • Item PLOP0609
ISBN 0-87322-609-7 • $18.95 ($27.95 Canadian)

Features 36 drills to help develop players' skills and explains how to develop a coaching philosophy, communicate on and off the field, and motivate players. Covers

bunting • baserunning • hitting • offensive strategies • defensive techniques at each position • defensive strategies • pitching

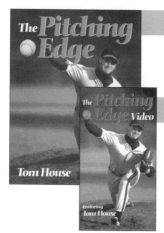

Tom House, PhD

Foreword by Nolan Ryan

1994 • Paper • 168 pp • Item PHOU0503
ISBN 0-87322-503-1 • $17.95 ($25.95 Canadian)

(54-minute videotape)

1995 • 1/2" VHS • Item MHOU0414
ISBN 0-87322-787-5 • $29.95 ($44.95 Canadian)

Special Book and Video Package
1/2" VHS and *The Pitching Edge* book
Item MHOU0420 • ISBN 0-87322-807-3
$44.95 ($67.50 Canadian)

This book is full of cutting-edge information for pitchers and coaches at every level. It covers the three keys to pitching success: technique, training, and thinking. For each segment of the pitch, it translates biomechanical principles into easy-to-understand information to improve pitching performance. Computer-generated illustrations highlight proper sequence and position throughout the pitching motion.

The companion videotape shows how pitching technique is taught, performed, and corrected for maximum efficiency and effectiveness on the mound.

Prices subject to change.
To request more information or to place an order, U.S. customers call
TOLL-FREE 1-800-747-4457. Customers outside the U.S. use the appropriate telephone
number/address shown in the front of this book.